D0287605

MIRACLES
of Renewal

WHEN MIRACLES HAPPEN
True Stories of God's Divine Touch

Edited by Mary Hollingsworth

Guideposts Books
Carmel, New York

Acknowledgments

Every attempt has been made to credit the sources of copyrighted material used in this book. If any such acknowledgment has been inadvertently omitted or miscredited, receipt of such information would be appreciated.

All material that originally appeared in Guideposts publicatons is reprinted with permission. Copyright © Guideposts, Carmel, NY.

Scripture quotations marked NCV are taken from *The Holy Bible*, New Century Version®, copyright © 1987, 1988, 1991 by Thomas Nelson, Inc. Used by permission. Scripture quotations marked NIV are taken from *The Holy Bible*, New International Version. Copyright © 1973, 1978, 1984, International Bible Society. Used by permission of Zondervan Bible Publishers. Quotations designated KJV are from the King James Version of the Bible. Quotations designated RSV are from the *Revised Standard Version of the Bible*, copyright © National Council of Churches of Christ in America. Used by permission. Quotations designated NRSV are from the New Revised Standard Version Bible, copyright © 1989, Division of Christian Education of the National Council of the Churches of Christ in the United States of America. Used by permission. All rights reserved.

"God's Perfect Timing" by Patricia Dunnick, "Life's Recipes" by Kimberly Ripley, and "The Gift" by Vicky Tapp published by permission from *Whispers from Heaven*, copyright © Publications International, Ltd. "Living Proof" found in *When There is No Miracle* by Robert Wise (Ventura, CA: Regal, 1977). "One Good Turn" found in *Miracles and Other Wonders* by Charles Sellier (New York: Random House, 1994). "So You Think You're a Stud" by Norris Burkes. Syndicated columnist with Gannett News Service. www.thechaplain.net. "Botta Bing, Botta Boom" excerpted from *In the Beginning...There Were No Diapers* by Tim Bete, ©2005. Used with permission of the publisher, Sorin Books, an imprint of Ave Maria Press, www.ave-mariapress.com. "One Small Loaf of Bread" by Kris Decker. "Treasure Hunting" by Cheryl Norwood, and "Internet Angels" by Susan Farr Fahneke from *God Allows U Turns* © 2002. Used by permission. www.GodAllowsUturns.com.

"Chocolate Delight" by Vicki P. Graham, "Two Step and Me" by Greg Asimakoupoulos, "When Dreams Come True at Sixty" by Christine Louise Hohlbaum, www.diaryofamother.com, "Lost and Found" by Mary Hollingsworth, "Die to Live" by Holly Baxley , "Pikes Peak Lightning" by Zarette Beard, "Pursuing Truth" by Ron Wheeler, www.ronwheeler.com, "When All Else Fails" by Glynnis Whitwer, "Epiphany" by Vicki P. Graham, "Peace Be Still" by Nika Maples, "A Child Sized Miracle" by Jamie Jarnigan Beavers, "Saved Twice" by Carly Boohm, are used by permission of the authors.

www.guideposts.org
(800) 431-2344
Guideposts Books & Inspirational Media Division

Illustrations by Ron Bucalo
Jacket design and photo by The DesignWorks Group, Inc.

Printed in the United States of America

Contents

Chapter 2 Learning What Matters Most

Chapter 3 Trusting God in Life's Storms

CHAPTER 4 DISCOVERING THE JOY OF TRUTH

CHAPTER 5 FINDING HOPE THROUGH DESPAIR

Introduction

Sometimes folks look in the mirror and see the years creeping up on them. A few laugh lines around the eyes. Hair that's thinning a bit. And sight that's not as sharp as it once was.

Still, those who are in tune with God are basically happy from day to day. Getting older isn't scary or frustrating to them; it's just a natural part of life. And those of us who are younger find great comfort in their obvious inward feeling of well-being, in spite of what their bodies may no longer be able to do.

It reminds me of the scripture that says, "We do not lose heart. Though outwardly we are wasting away, yet inwardly we are being renewed day by day" (2 Corinthians 4:16, NIV).

Renewal! It's definitely a gift from God. We see it every spring when the trees bud out in verdant green and the flowers burst into vibrant colors. We see it in the dimples and captivating smile of a new baby. We see it in the radiant faces of people in love, both young and old. And we hear it in exuberant songs of praise of the God who renews us inwardly with His Spirit, His grace, and His joy.

Miracles of Renewal is a wonderful collection of heartwarming stories that remind us of God's constant ability to energize and encourage us, even in the midst of life's storms and trials. He is the miracle of light in our darkness, of hope in our despair, of joy in our sorrow. And He brings us quiet peace when life feels as if it's spinning madly out of control.

In Chapter 1, "Returning from Darkness to Light," when a young girl has to move away from her friends, God lifts her spirits by surprising her with Easter eggs in a park. God's perfect timing helps Patricia to break the ice with her neighbor and give her a reason to live. And Kris finds hope through the gift of a single loaf of bread.

"Learning What Matters Most" is the theme of Chapter 2, where Nancy is caught in a tornado and discovers the miracle of God's love through her driveway angel. After sixty years of hoping and dreaming, Barbara is surprised by God with her one true love. And Kimberly discovers what's really important when she inherits her grandmother's recipe box.

Chapter 3 reveals how we can begin "Trusting God in Life's Storms." When little Justin is killed by lightning, his father rediscovers God through the love of His people. A blind man experiences transformation when he must rescue his blind neighbor from a fire. And disheartened after losing everything in Hurricane Katrina, a woman finds herself in God's presence through small miraculous signs.

Chapter 4 includes stories about "Discovering the Joy of Truth," such as the one about Ron, who finally gets what he's always wanted by giving it up. Jody learns to accept her debilitating epilepsy and herself; then she realizes her fear of living has vanished too. And Joseph's life is saved by a mysterious waitress and a piece of apple pie.

"Finding Hope Through Despair" is Chapter 5's focus where Susan experiences a brain tumor and learns that life is not a race but a journey. Internet angels give hope and courage to a woman whose sister is losing her battle with cancer. And Joel's prayer life is renewed when his teenage daughter is in a critical car accident.

The next time you look in the mirror, see if the God of renewal is looking back through your sparkling eyes. Ask Him to fill your heart with joy and to help you feel "new every morning." His love and care are miraculous buoys for our lives—they keep us afloat in the turbulent seas we sail from birth until death. And they make the journey a joy and a delight.

MARY HOLLINGSWORTH

MIRACLES
of Renewal

CHAPTER 1

Returning from Darkness to Light

LORD, you give light to my lamp. The LORD brightens the darkness around me. (2 Samuel 22:29, NCV).

When the darkness of life closes in around us, as it inevitably does from time to time because that's just how life is, we are fearful. Like a small child who is afraid of the dark and cries out for his father to come and sit with him, we want our Father to walk with us through the shadows. We long for Him to turn on the light and chase away the frightening moments of life. And because He loves us so, He comes. He stays with us, and He lights our way to the end of the valley. It is His miracle of renewal for us.

The New House on Celeste Avenue

MAUREEN KUEHNE

I was curled up with a Nancy Drew mystery on the big screened porch of our upstairs duplex, shaded by the live oak trees that made Carrollton Avenue the prettiest promenade in all New Orleans. I could spend a whole day up there reading and watching streetcars lumber along the tracks on the neutral ground across the street.

"Get your shoes on," Mama said, suddenly before me, her belly full with the baby who was threatening to ruin my life. "We're going to see the new house."

To accommodate our growing family, we were moving to the suburbs that spring of 1957. Never mind that I was only eleven—I was a city girl, thank you, and I didn't want to leave our castlelike duplex. Nothing would be the same. My two younger siblings didn't care that we were being dragged away. When Mama promised lots of open space for riding bikes and a year-round snowball stand, Barbara Anne, eight, and Michael, five, were sold.

I made a face and took my time slipping on my sandals. "Bring your library book," Mama said. "You can read on the way."

We piled into the car and fought over who got the window seats, then Daddy drove us past the library, an antebellum red-brick building with white columns and a wide stairway, where my friend the librarian always held the brand-new Nancy Drews aside for me. We passed the grocery with the best candy selection ever, and the dance studio where I took jazz and tap with Mr. Tony. How could I leave all this behind?

I closed my eyes and listened to a streetcar clang in the distance. When I was outside the house, that bell always set my legs in motion. I'd run up our stoop, pull open the door, race upstairs and around the worn-smooth banister, through the living room, out the tall French doors, and onto the screened porch. If I got there before the streetcar passed, I was the winner.

Now the streetcar's clang only made me feel sad. My Sunday school teacher had told us the week before that Easter was just around the corner, and with Jesus in our hearts, we had so much to look forward to, things we couldn't even begin to imagine. But I had no place in my heart for Easter joy, not when I was about to move and leave behind everything I loved in this world.

"That's it, four-twenty Celeste Avenue," Daddy said, pointing to the house as it came into view. I'd never seen a house with no porch on it. Where would I read?

Michael and Barbara Anne zoomed in to call their bedrooms. It was all the same to me: The house, inside and out, was utterly charmless. Which is exactly how I was now acting, leaning arms-crossed against the kitchen counter.

Mama came over to me and cupped her hand under my chin, gently raising my eyes to meet hers. She said, "Change can be hard, honey, I know. But sometimes it can be the start of something wonderful. Give it a chance, would you? For me?"

"Okay, Mama," I said, "I'll try to like it just a little bit."

The moving van came the first Friday in March, and just before Daddy locked up the duplex, I heard a clang in the distance. "Wait!" I yelled, racing up the stoop, inside, up the stairs and around the banister, through the living room, out the French doors, and onto the screened porch. I looked up, breathless . . . Victory! I waved as the streetcar moved past and out of sight, then went downstairs to get in the car.

My heart broke as we drove away. *Jesus, please help me find some Easter joy. I promised Mama I'd try, but I don't know where to start.*

Nevertheless, Barbara Anne and Michael and I got up early the next morning and ate cereal in front of the cartoons while our parents slept. Daddy had been working extra hard to be able to afford this move, and they both deserved a good rest.

"Let's ride bikes to the park," I suggested. By 7 A.M. we were already dressed and out the door. This was a big deal, even I had to admit. We weren't allowed to ride our bikes to Audubon Park in New Orleans.

Side by side the three of us pedaled along leisurely, smack in the middle of the street.

"Lights!" Barbara Anne shouted at the end of our block. Giant silver lamps cast a wide, white hazy light over the ball field just ahead.

"Last one there's a rotten egg!" Michael called out.

We reached the ball field in a three-way tie and hopped off our banana seats. All of us stood straddling our bikes, staring at the grassy green baseball diamond. Large painted tin eggs were scattered about—dozens of them all over the field, as if it were one gigantic Easter basket. My brother and sister and I were silent. Who were all these eggs for? And where had they come from? I felt like Nancy Drew come to life.

Michael finally dropped his bike and walked up to an egg with yellow chicks painted all over it.

"No!" I shouted. "Don't touch anything. Guard the eggs. I'll be right back." I hopped back on my seat and pedaled home as fast as I could.

I went around to Mama's side of the bed. "Mama," I whispered, "wake up. There's a mystery at the park." Mama leaned up on her elbows while I described what we'd found. "Can we bring some of the eggs home, do you think? Can we?"

"Why sure, honey. They must be there for the taking."

"Thanks!" I said and ran back out to my bike. From half a block away I shouted to Barbara Anne and Michael, "Mama says it's okay!" We stuffed eggs under our shirts and one under the chin, and carefully walked our bikes home.

"My goodness!" Mama said when we lined all the eggs up on the table. "Have you ever seen such a thing?"

Each egg was painted differently, and Mama picked up the one decorated with tulips. She ran her finger along a seam in the middle. "They must open like those little plastic ones from the dime store," she said. Mama separated the halves and out fell a piece of paper, fortune-cookie-style. We all crowded around to see what it said, but Mama read it aloud. "Good for a ten-dollar set of tools from Bud's Hardware. Compliments of WYLD, New Orleans Radio."

I opened the next egg: "Get a free permanent wave at Shirley's Hair Salon." Barbara Anne was entitled to groceries from the Hill Store, and Michael got a candy certificate.

We let Daddy open the last two eggs in bed—flowers and an oil change! "This is great," Dad said. "Every little bit helps right now." We tossed around the big eggs and paraded around our new house. It seemed like we were celebrating Christmas at Eastertime.

Later in the day we went for a drive around the town and got to know some of the local merchants. We stopped for snowballs at the year-round stand, then happened upon the parish bookmobile, where I found a complete, illustrated set of the Nancy Drew mysteries. Back in the car we sang loud to WYLD with the windows rolled down.

As we pulled under the carport we heard the announcer say the WYLD Easter Bunny had made an early visit to parks around New Orleans.

"We never would've been first at Audubon Park," I said. "We're lucky we live out here."

Mama turned around slowly, a smile lighting up her face and making a wide-open space in my heart for joy. The new house was full of surprises and so far it was only Easter.

God's Perfect Timing

PATRICIA DUNNICK

One Sunday in church the pastor read Revelation 4:11 (KJV): "Thou art worthy, O Lord, to receive glory and honour and power: for thou hast created all things, and for thy pleasure they are and were created."

I accepted the challenge for our new neighbors, Belinda and Chet. "Father," I prayed, "I don't have anything in common with Belinda, but I'd like the opportunity to witness to her. Help me to bring honor and glory and pleasure to you. I pray that Belinda can know you as her Father. In Jesus's name, Amen."

I could sense that Belinda didn't want to get involved with us, even though I always made a point to be friendly, greeting her and her daughters. Many times I'd go to the fence and make small talk with her. I prayed for the Lord to soften her heart and give me an "in" so I could get to know her better.

One day while I was sitting at the kitchen table, sewing a swimming suit for Betty, our ten-year-old, someone knocked at the door. I yelled, "Come in!"

Belinda opened the door and held out a measuring

cup, explaining that she'd run out of sugar and had to hurry back since the twins were in bed.

Dawn, our thirteen-year-old, quickly got the sugar for her. Belinda watched me sewing the swimsuit, and suddenly, her voice changed. "I didn't know you liked to sew," she remarked.

"I've always made Betty's swimsuits," I replied. Betty smiled.

"I sew for the department store displays!" Belinda said proudly.

"Are those yours? Wow, they're good! I can't sew nearly as well as you," I replied.

That broke the ice! Belinda asked Dawn if she'd watch the twins. She wanted to help me sew Betty's suit! Soon our children were playing together, and we were exchanging recipes.

I continued to pray for Belinda and her family each day. I asked God to tell me when I could share his plan of salvation with her, and I waited for a sign that the time was right.

One afternoon, while I was washing the lunch dishes, I heard, "Go now and take your Bible." I quickly grabbed my Bible and told Dawn it was time for me to go. The children knew what I was doing and were excited. It was time!

I walked through the gate and knocked at the back door. Belinda answered, and by her expression I could tell the girls were asleep.

She opened the door and simply said, "I want what you have!"

Startled at her statement, I looked in at her lavish home and replied, "What do I have?"

"You have peace, and I don't. Chet and I have five Bibles on our headboard, and at night we read from them but none of it makes any sense to us."

I asked if I could come in. We went into the living room, sat down, and opened the Bible I'd brought with me. I had her read the story of the creation, then about Adam's sin, then I showed her the Christmas story and the story of Easter. As she read, I could see she was beginning to understand some of it. Then I explained to her that having peace only comes when you ask Jesus Christ into your life. I also told her that to make a decision like that was between her and God and that I didn't need to be there. She said she wanted to keep reading and would think things over. I left my Bible with her, went home, and prayed for her.

Around suppertime the door sprang open, and Belinda came rushing up to me joyfully saying, "When Chet came home he asked me, 'What has happened to you?' He noticed, without me even telling him!"

Belinda was anxious to learn more about the Bible and get involved in a prayer group, so we decided to start a neighborhood Bible study as soon as possible. Belinda wanted to visit all the neighbors and invite them herself. My sister-in-law, Kate, volunteered to give a series of talks about marriage, and my mom said she would teach the children at my house while we met at Belinda's.

The Bible study was a huge success for everyone involved. It helped to bring our neighborhood together, and even more important, we were able to pray for a lot of families and bring about change in many women's lives.

At our third meeting, Kate decided to go around the table and have each woman give her testimony about how she had found the Lord. Kate gave hers first, since she was the leader. Then another neighbor spoke, and then came Belinda. I smiled and settled back, thinking that I knew exactly what she was going to say. She looked over at me and began, "I was so unhappy . . . I had decided to commit suicide."

I sat straight up, and my mouth fell open out of sheer surprise. She had never told me anything about this!

"I had it planned for months," she continued. "I would get the girls napping, and when they were in a deep sleep, I would get in the car and drive off the Highway 61 bridge. I had driven past there a hundred times, and I noticed a certain spot where a car could go off and no one could see it from the road. I had just gotten the girls down for their nap one afternoon when Patricia knocked at the door. I didn't know who it was, but whoever it was, they were interrupting my plans! When I saw Patricia there, I opened the door, and before

I really knew what I was doing, I shouted, 'I want what you have!' Patricia came in and showed me passages from the Bible that I hadn't understood before. She explained to me that the only way to find true inner peace was to give my life to Jesus. Then she left me, and that's when I talked to God and asked Jesus into my life. I have had genuine inner peace ever since."

I sat there in shock, as most of the women did. I don't remember what I said when it was my turn. I could only reflect on God's timing, and on how much he loves each of us and knows our hearts. To this day I stand amazed at all the Lord wants to do, if only we are willing and ready.

I've definitely learned one thing: God is never late!

Living Proof

ROBERT L. WISE

My six-year-old son, Tate, had a shattered, tumorous leg. He would not even have made it to age six without God's gracious intervention.

Shortly after his birth, we began to be aware of an unusual skin color. Since he had Indian background, we assumed he was going to be an unusually dark "red-skinned" child. But the skin color was strange. Gradually the shading took on a more yellowish cast.

One morning as the sunlight streamed in striking his small, innocent face, we discovered his eyes were turning yellow. He was jaundiced! Being so close we hadn't caught the subtlety of change. He was turning yellow by degrees.

Immediately the tiny bundle was rushed for medical examination. The grave response of the doctor spoke volumes. He quietly called the hospital and we went straight to the surgicial floor.

A congenital liver defect was forcing bile into his system. The facts were simple. At six weeks of age and under six pounds in weight, surgery was a complete hazard. It would be like operating on a rabbit. The chances were nil. But that wasn't the worst news. To the doctor's knowledge, no one had ever survived this condition. Generally an infant wasted away.

I was too shocked even to worry about the "why" questions. I found myself walking dazed through a maze of unknown emotions. I was too young and out of touch with my feelings even to know how to respond.

My wife and I were young Christians and not sure how to proceed. Somewhere we had heard we were to trust and pray. We did.

That evening I insisted my wife go home. I would spend the night with this baby. I felt I could "take it" better. Little did I know!

As the night wore on I went through the funeral and the burial a hundred times. Intermittently I prayed. By morning I was a basket case.

Barbara arrived very early. Unlike me, she was quite calm and composed. Her simple faith had given her an entirely different experience through the dark hours. After praying she had sensed a great calm and assurance that allowed her to fall asleep. In that peaceful sleep a clear dream took shape. She could vividly remember dreaming that the surgery completely corrected the condition. In detail she described what would happen and how a by-pass would be constructed. Carefully she shared that he would live and would be a special child.

It was all too much for me. I couldn't get what she was saying. My vision had been an open grave with the family standing beside a small casket. When they came with the long, black surgical cart, I was overwhelmed.

Three hours later, the doctor burst into the room. He was elated! He couldn't believe it! Obviously the surgical success was a first for him. He was amazed with the result. As he carefully shared his discovery of how they had constructed a by-pass for the bile duct, it was like watching a movie. I had heard the exact description three hours before.

God did a special thing in our lives. That little boy was living proof of His miraculous power!

Do I believe in miracles? You bet!

One Small Loaf of Bread

KRIS DECKER

Man does not live on bread alone" (Luke 4:4, NIV). It was a verse I'd heard all my life. But eleven years ago I learned a person could live quite well on bread, especially when it comes from a divine source.

I was only thirty years old at the time, living in the rubble of what had once been my carefully constructed life. My six-year marriage had crumbled, I was raising my daughter alone, and I was working two jobs to support our little household. Anxiety and fear settled over me like a cloud of ashes as my bank balance dwindled and my debts mounted. Just when I thought things could not disintegrate any further, my ex-husband stopped paying child support. No matter how many hours I worked, I couldn't earn enough to make ends meet without that monthly check.

Although I was on my own financially, I received emotional support from my new friends—people I'd recently met in a twelve-step group, along with my neighbors, all of whom just happened to be Christians. They told me if I turned my life over to the care of my loving Father in heaven, He would help me. I had to admit it sounded good. But like those ads I'd seen posted on power-line poles—"Lose 30 pounds in 30 days"—it seemed too good to be true.

I moved forward cautiously. Unlike others who describe the beginning of their spiritual journey as a leap of faith, mine was more like tiptoeing toward trust. Warily, I accepted my neighbor's invitation to attend her church.

"Just one time," I told her, fearing entrapment, brainwashing, or some other kind of manipulation lying in wait.

"Of course," she said. "No pressure."

Much to my surprise, it was a pleasant experience. The people were kind, and the doctrine made sense. Everything should have clicked right into place, but it didn't. My heart was shut tight, double-bolted with the security alarm fully activated. I was afraid. What if I did turn my life over to God and declare Jesus as my Savior? Did He really care about what happened to me? And who was I to even ask for help anyway?

Then a small loaf of bread arrived.

"At long last, the famine has ended! Look what I got today," I announced to my friends, dropping the freshly baked bread onto the table with a thud. They all stared, confused by the roll of my eyes and the sarcastic tone in my voice. "I got it from that church I've gone to a couple of times," I explained. "You know, the one my neighbor invited me to? They give this to all the new attendees." I laughed scornfully. "If this is God's way of feeding us, we're going to starve within a week."

It was like the worst kind of cruel joke. Only the day before, my mailbox had bulged with bills, each demanding immediate payment. The mortgage company, the electric company, and the city water co-op all tossed out threats like hand grenades: foreclosure, disconnection, discontinued service. Worse still, I didn't know where I was going to get money for food. Our refrigerator and cupboards echoed from bareness, and I wouldn't get a paycheck for another ten days. That small loaf of bread seemed to mock my situation. I could lose everything, and if this was God, why was He sending me this one pathetic, puny loaf of bread?

My friend Beth reached across the table and patted my hand. "Maybe this is God's way of letting you know He's going to take care of you," she said kindly.

"Yeah, right," I muttered, slumping down into my chair like a petulant teenager. I had plenty of reasons to feel cynical about getting assistance from God.

It wasn't that I didn't believe in Him. If anything, I believed too well the lessons I'd learned as a child in our "religious" home, memorizing doctrine that taught me I had to earn the trip to heaven. All of my life I'd felt like a kid selling candy for a school fund-raiser, never quite producing enough good acts, and ultimately falling short of my quota and the grand prize: an all-expense paid trip to paradise. Even more discouraging was the belief that God didn't really know or care about me personally, or so I'd been told. He was just too busy with more important things, they said—like wars and floods and the Super Bowl.

"Well, if God doesn't care about me," I'd decided, "then I am certainly not going to care about Him." And I closed and locked the door to my heart. There was no way He could get in, because only I possessed the key.

Later that evening, after I'd taken my bread home and tucked my daughter into bed, I sat down to think. One of my friends had given me a Bible promise book, which lists biblical promises related specifically to issues we face every day. I began glancing though it.

I'll just see what God has to say about money, I thought. The defiant part of me wanted to challenge this seemingly foolish belief, while another part hoped to find some kind of fiscal Charles Schwab–type advice in those pages. Randomly I flipped open the book, not to "money" as I'd intended but to a section on "faith." The verses all but jumped out of the book and shouted in my face.

"Believe in the Lord Jesus, and you will be saved—you and your household" (Acts 16:31).

"I have come into the world as a light, so that no one who believes in me should stay in darkness" (John 12:46).

"Then Jesus declared, 'I am the bread of life. He who comes to me will never go hungry, and he who believes in me will never be thirsty'" (John 6:35).

I know God's voice is almost always a still, small one—a whisper, a breeze, the gentlest of nudges. But that night was different. Like Saul of Tarsus, I needed to be blinded by a magnificent flash of light in order to see the truth. And I was, for there before me, spelled out in black and white, were the answers to every one of my problems—the house payment, the electric bill, the water bill, and food. If God had taken out a full-page ad in the *New York Times*, His message could not have been more obvious. The very thought of it took my breath away. At long last, the door to my heart flew open and completely off its hinges.

I sank to my knees, and for the first time in my life, I cried out to God for His help. For the first time in my life, I really believed God heard.

Two days later, I received a phone call from the pastor at the "Loaf of Bread" church. He said he wanted to meet me. We agreed he would come to my home the following evening.

When he arrived, I barely managed to open the door before he began to speak. He was grinning and nearly danced his way into my living room.

"I received a very clear message from the Holy Spirit concerning you," he said, smiling. "Here."

He pushed a piece of paper into my hand. Confused and a bit frightened, I slowly unfolded the paper, half expecting one of those pink phone messages one gets at the office, "While You Were Out, the Holy Spirit Called." But it wasn't that at all. It was a check for $1,000—the exact amount of money I needed to pay all of my bills and buy food.

The pastor told me it wasn't a loan, and there were no strings attached. I didn't need to do anything at all to deserve or earn this money. It was a gift, just like God's love. Just like Jesus' sacrifice on the cross.

I don't remember much else about that night. I think I was in shock, dazzled at the thought that the Creator of the universe did in fact love and care about me. Me! How could Someone so divine love me?

Even after all this time, I am still amazed by God's grace. But what's most remarkable is that God's intercession didn't end with the delivery of that check. Two months after I received it, I lost my house to foreclosure, my car to the junk pile, and my jobs to cutbacks and layoffs.

Like any good Father, God wanted not only to care for me but also to teach and guide me. Once I truly believed I wasn't too insignificant for God to love, then I needed to build on my faith, lean on God instead of the world, and trust He would always take care of me, even in the worst of times.

And He did. Because even after I lost all my material possessions, I discovered my life didn't end. In fact, the more I lost, the richer I became. When I surrendered my life's journey to God, He set me gently upon a new path and blessed me abundantly. Within two years after receiving the loaf of bread, I married a man rooted in his faith and belief in God. God gave us a second beautiful child and provided me with one miraculous opportunity after another to complete my education and begin a new career. He presented me with a quality of life, happiness, and peace that could only come from a benevolent Father who, in His infinite wisdom, knew all along what was best for me. The kind of Father who could take one small loaf of bread and feed me with it for the rest of my life.

My Best Role

TOM STREET

Turning sixteen was no big deal. Nothing was. I'd just started high school, and life was far from thrilling. My 200-plus pounds got me on the football team, and I showed up for practice. So what? It didn't make me a star, on or off the field. Girls wouldn't give me the time of day. I just blended into the crowd, going this way or that, taking the path of least resistance.

One afternoon, out in the school parking lot, someone clapped me on the back. It was a teacher, suit and tie—the whole deal.

"Chuck Ramsey," he said, putting out his hand. "I'm the drama teacher." He had a happy look on his face, like it really meant something to be a drama teacher. "Would you like to be in my class?"

Give me a break. "Try it," he said. "What have you got to lose?" The path of least resistance. I followed him to the classroom. I saw three other guys—and maybe forty girls. I signed up.

That's how it started, in Farmington, New Mexico, in 1980. Chuck Ramsey put me onstage with a girl and told me to improvise a love scene. Pretty funny. I'd never even called a girl for a date.

"Hey, doll," I said, clowning it up, "call me Romeo." A strange thing happened. Kids laughed. I kept it up, saying whatever came to mind. The girl played along.

"Great!" said Mr. Ramsey. I saw that happy look again. He meant it.

Mr. Ramsey cast me in lots of plays. We did Shakespeare, for real, and old-time melodramas. I sang in *The Pajama Game*. I finally understood why Mr. Ramsey had that happy look. Acting was fun. I decided that for an old guy in his thirties, Mr. Ramsey was pretty cool. But one day in class he went into shock and collapsed on the floor. There was something about our teacher we hadn't known: he had diabetes.

Soon after I graduated, Mr. Ramsey stopped teaching because of his health. He came to see me in every play I did at our local college, and we became friends. "Please call me Chuck," he said one night. "I'm not your teacher anymore."

"You'll always be my teacher," I said. He'd taught me that life could be a big deal. And now I knew what I wanted to do with my life: be an actor.

I often dropped by to see Chuck and his wife, Patti. His condition worsened, and he was put on a waiting list for a kidney transplant. Doctors eventually found a donor for him, and things went well for a while. They adopted a son, Zach. Then Zach caught chicken pox, and Chuck got it too. The disease wrecked his immune system. Patti called me late one night. "Can you come over? She asked. "Chuck may not make it."

I was stunned when I walked into their house. Chuck was hunched over in a wheelchair, skin and bones. I knelt down to see his face. The happy look was gone. *God, what can I do to help this man who helped me so much?*

Chuck came within a thread of dying, but doctors pulled him through. He went on dialysis and enjoyed every minute of watching Zach grow up. I worked different jobs, but acting was still the one thing I really wanted in life. I read the Hollywood trade papers for auditions.

One day I raced over to see Chuck. "Guess what?" I said. "I got a part in a movie!" Chuck's whole face wrinkled up into a grin.

"Way to go, Tom!" he said.

Each time I saw Chuck, he seemed less like his old self. The dialysis was rough on him. He was always weak and his color was bad. His eyesight was failing. I'd done some reading about diabetes, and I knew that dialysis couldn't remove all the toxins in his body. *What he really needs is another transplant*, I thought. But when I mentioned it, he shrugged it off. "I'm doing okay," he said. I knew my drama teacher was acting.

But his battles weren't over. Patti Ramsey died of cancer in 2000. Zach was eleven. "He wakes me up every night," Chuck confided. "He wants to be sure I'm not dead too." In reality, Chuck was dead or wanted to be.

"Don't forget," I said, 'We are such stuff as dreams are made of!'" I couldn't believe I was quoting Shakespeare. Before I met Chuck, I barely knew who Shakespeare was! This man had changed my life. I had to do something to help him. "Chuck," I said, "I want to give you a kidney."

He wouldn't listen. "Try it," I said. "What have you got to lose?" It was exactly what he'd said to me years before when he first dragged me onto the stage. He gave in. We had tests done at the dialysis center.

"I'm sorry," the nurse said. "You're not a match."

I was quiet, crushed with disappointment. Then I heard something. Not a voice, exactly, but a stirring in my heart: "The tests are wrong," I said.

"It's okay," Chuck said. "We tried." The nurse looked at me like I was out of my mind. "Think of Shakespeare," I said to Chuck. 'There are more things in heaven and earth than are dreamt of in your philosophy.'"

Chuck didn't talk about it anymore. He stayed on dialysis. But I couldn't stop thinking of that stirring in my heart. One night, surfing the Internet, I came across a site for the Mayo Clinic in Rochester, Minnesota. The clinic had developed a new procedure called positive crossmatch transplants. Chuck could receive a kidney from a living donor with a different blood type. A donor like me.

"Chuck!" I shouted into the phone. "Wake up. We can do it!"

"That's too much to ask," Chuck said. It took three months to change his mind. We sent the blood tests to the Mayo Clinic by overnight mail. My phone rang a week later. "Mr. Street," the doctor said, "I have good news. You and Mr. Ramsey don't need the positive crossmatch procedure. The two of you are a perfect match."

"What do you mean?" I asked. The doctor responded: "The previous tests you had were wrong." That stirring in my heart was an angel speaking to me.

Chuck and I went to the Mayo Clinic last April. The morning after the transplant, I walked down the hospital corridor. Chuck lighted up when I appeared in the doorway. His skin glowed, more normal in color than it had been in years. I saw that happy look on his face I hadn't seen for so long.

We're both doing great. "I got a good part," I told Chuck. "Maybe a whole minute on screen." He laughed. How good it is to hear him laugh. Just like the old days when he first pushed me onto the stage. Shakespeare said, "One man in his time plays many parts." Chuck changed my life. My best role has been to help change his.

Chocolate Delight

VICKI P. GRAHAM

For weeks our church had been preparing and praying for the annual Youth Encounter, a three-day event held at a beautiful lodge in the mountains. Classes would be held for some forty boys and girls, recreational activities would abound, and food would be abundant. And the highlight would be the nightly praise and worship.

Youth encounters were sponsored every quarter by our church and many teenagers turned their lives around due to these events. Some town kids had never been in a church nor knew much about Jesus Christ and His miracles until they were invited by our church youth to experience the intense yet fun weekend

Thus, many of the teens were seriously praying and many were fasting as they interceded for their friends who would be attending. And they were careful to include their teachers and leaders in their prayers for miracles to occur at the encounter.

The youth minister, Travis Williams, took the preparation one step further. He promised God a twenty-one-day fast that would end the day the group boarded the bus to go to the mountains.

Now Travis loved to eat. In fact, next to singing and playing music, he probably liked eating more than almost anything. Therefore, disciplining himself to eat nothing but water was an incredible sacrifice, a fact that did not go unnoticed by the kids for whom he was interceding. Many were watching him carefully to see if he would break. The last week of his fast some of the seriously devoted youth followed his example and also fasted.

The last day of Travis's fast, one of the biggest and most beautiful weddings ever held at our church occurred. The granddaughter of one of our longtime church leaders was the bride, and the family went all out to make the event unforgettable. The bride was lovely and the music wonderful. But when the ceremony was over and the doors were opened to the fellowship hall, Travis couldn't believe his eyes.

The tables were laden with gorgeous foods. The smells were mouthwatering. For someone who hadn't eaten in twenty days the temptation to break his fast one day early was tremendous. We all watched Travis's reaction to the vast array of goodies. You could almost hear a group sigh of relief as the teens saw him shake his head and turn away from the tables.

When Travis resisted the main dishes and turned away, he ran right into the table with the bride's sumptuous wedding cake. The reaction of us spectators was almost like that at a sporting event; we collectively sighed, "Oh, no!"

"Ah," we breathed as Travis stepped away. But "No," we moaned. *Get out of here Satan,* I thought. Travis had turned toward the groom's table, on top of which was the most humongous chocolate cake most of us had ever seen. It was probably at least sixteen inches tall, slathered in two kinds of chocolate icing, and covered with chocolate shavings. Crushed nuts and chocolate sprinkles added an irresistible touch.

But, would Travis be able to resist? I knew from the kids observing him that they were praying for a miracle. The adults didn't notice what was going on, but the tension among the youth, many of whom had been his charges for years, was almost palpable. They wanted their friend and mentor to have the victory.

Then it happened. Travis turned his back on the temptation and walked determinedly out of the reception!

Low fives and grins all around. It was too formal and dignified an affair for high fives and shouts of victory. Travis had won and we shared the pleasure. The teens were as pleased as if they had won the war themselves.

Three of us did the cooking for the youth encounter. That chore entailed working up the menus and shopping. Of course, hamburgers, pizza, tacos, and bountiful breakfasts were the musts. And sweets were all important to keep these kids energized. We were lingering after the reception was over when the mother of the bride came up and asked if she could donate to our efforts.

"No one touched the chocolate cake," she informed us. "I wonder if you could use it at the encounter?"

Could we ever! Who could turn down a slice of that paradise? Well, yes, Travis had turned it down, but we knew that was a God thing. We boxed it and toted it to our horde of supplies we'd be hauling to the mountains the next day. Almost everyone had departed and we were adults, but we still high-fived and congratulated ourselves for this delicious addition to our menu.

Friday evening found us cooking a great supper for the kids. After we cleaned up, our lead cook called us to a huddle.

"Guess what," she said. "Tomorrow is Travis's birthday. I brought candles for that chocolate cake he wanted so much. Let's keep it a surprise and present it after lunch tomorrow."

What a great idea! We hid the cake in the recesses of the wonderful camp kitchen and agreed it would be such great fun to present it the next day.

The next morning we could hardly wait. We made it through breakfast. Many of the kids had never eaten an omelet, let alone seen one cooked. They were mesmerized as they filed through the kitchen and watched my husband expertly flip their orders. It was a great lesson for the boys to watch a male chef. Those who were veterans of youth encounters were telling their first-time buddies, "Wait till you see Roger toss those fried eggs in the air and flip the omelets."

Finally lunchtime arrived. We located some of the leaders and told them we wanted to honor Travis with a surprise birthday party before the afternoon session. They agreed to gather all forty of the kids, not a small task, and have them waiting in the meeting room before someone would bring Travis in from the basketball game going on outside.

Try placing thirty-seven candles on a cake that weighs a ton, getting them lit, and lugging it into the hall just as Travis was escorted in. The cake was blazing, the kids were singing "Happy Birthday" as Travis entered. His eyes filled with tears, his mouth was a huge grin as he looked at the crowd gathered to honor him.

And then he saw the cake.

"It's a miracle," he whispered. "It's a miracle," he said even louder. "You don't know how badly I wanted to break my fast a day early and have a piece of my favorite dessert.

"God is so good," he said tearfully. "Here's the whole thing set right before me. God is always on time."

There wasn't a dry eye in the room. We all rejoiced in the miracle God had presented Travis. And we all rejoiced as we shared the chocolate delight.

CHAPTER 2

Learning What Matters Most

Do not conform any longer to the pattern of this world, but be transformed by the renewing of your mind. (Romans 12:2, NIV)

Life is full of the mundane and day-to-day trivia. We tend to major in minors and concentrate our thoughts and efforts on the elements of living that are just passing fads or fancies. God calls us to do what matters most in life—to spend our days glorifying and praising Him so that others can find their way to Him as well. He calls us to reflect His light into the shadowy corners of our hopeless world and to show His love to the loveless.

Our Sanctuary

NANCY OLTMAN

On a sunny May Sunday afternoon last year, I stood on the front porch, watching the birds and squirrels flit through the trees. More than 150 trees of all kinds shaded our property—maple, sycamore, hickory, redbud, elm, and mulberry. In summer the foliage was so thick you couldn't see our house. We put a stone angel by the driveway to mark the spot, lest someone miss it. "God is here," the angel seemed to say, and I believed that was true. When I returned home from another trying day at work, I'd turn at our driveway angel, ride in among the trees, and feel at peace.

The radio had warned of a tornado, with hail as big as golf balls, but the sky was a clear bright blue. The Ozarks of southwestern Missouri are known for tornadoes, but in the years the kids and I had lived here we'd been lucky not to have experienced one.

My daughter called from her friend's house, a mile away. Naomi was fifteen, still my baby girl. "They say I should stay put," she said. "We're going down to the basement where it's safe." I looked out the window. The sun was still shining. It didn't seem possible there could be a storm of any kind.

"Okay, Naomi. You do what they say."

I went outside to call my son in: "Ryan!" My twenty-one-year-old was in his shop by the barn, working on a four-wheeler with his best friend, Briceton, and their girlfriends. "A tornado's threatening!" I shouted. The kids stepped out the door. "There's hail too! Put those cars in the barn now."

"Sure, Mom," Ryan said. He'd seen a hail storm once, over at the quarry where he worked. All the cars' windshields had been smashed to bits.

The kids took care of the cars, then joined me out on the porch. "It's not dark enough for a tornado," Ryan said.

"But listen," said Briceton. "Sirens."

He was a local boy, and he had seen his share of tornadoes. Now that he mentioned it, I could hear the faint sounds of the sirens mounted in town that warned people of the impending danger of an approaching storm.

"Whoa!" shouted Ryan. "Here it comes!"

Chunks of ice suddenly hit the porch roof and bounced off the steps. The sky was clear, but something like a dark wall approached from the southwest. Then I heard the sound, unlike anything I'd ever heard in my life. A thundering, pounding sound, as if a giant were striding toward us, destroying the earth in his path.

"We'll take shelter in the bathroom," Briceton said. I

looked at him. "No window," he said, "and it's built solid." He seemed to know what he was talking about. We hurried off the porch. Five of us crowded into our tiny bathroom, huddled together like a big human ball. If only my daughter were here too . . .

Then it came. Roaring. Ripping. Crashing. Whirling wind shrieked around us. Trees thundered to the ground. My ears hurt from the noise.

I yelled, "Time to pray," and I prayed with my whole heart. "Dear Lord, keep the kids safe. Please watch over Naomi."

The walls shuddered as a tree fell. Each moment hung on forever. One of the girls was next to me, and I pulled her close, hoping, praying someone was protecting Naomi in her friend's basement.

Slowly, finally, the noise died away. The terrifying sounds stopped. It was strangely quiet. Then Briceton said, "I think it's safe now."

Ryan opened the door. Nothing could have prepared me for what I saw. Or what I didn't see. The land, once rich with forest, was stripped bare of trees as far as I could see. My sanctuary—destroyed. The roofs of the house, shop, and barn were gone. Flattened. All that was left standing were the walls of the bathroom where we had found shelter.

The five of us emerged without a scratch. It seemed a miracle. But what about everyone else, our neighbors . . .

Naomi! I headed down the hill, climbing over trees, to find her. *Please, Lord, let me hold my baby again*. The kids instinctively knew where I was going, and they followed.

"Watch out for the power lines!" Briceton shouted.

Sirens pierced the air. Ryan finally got through to Naomi on his cell phone. "She's on her way," Ryan said. "She's fine."

As I waited on the road, breathing hard, I saw our driveway angel. My heart wanted to break. It can't be true. The tornado had ripped the wings off our angel. Torn them completely off. All around me once-proud trees lay on the ground. Our house was in ruins, the land barren. In a terrible moment of time, everything was gone. Everything.

Then I saw Naomi running toward me along the road. I pulled her into my arms. She looked over my shoulder at the nothingness beyond.

"It's gone," she cried. "Our house. The trees. It's all gone." I could feel my daughter's heart beating close to mine. The daughter I feared might perish in the storm. The daughter I feared I might never see again. Yet here she was with me and my son, safe in my arms. My family had been spared. We would all go to sleep tonight and wake in the morning. Surely there were many families who wouldn't know such a blessing.

"We're all still here," I whispered in Naomi's ear. "And so is God. We haven't lost anything to speak of. We haven't lost what matters most."

We turned to walk up the driveway, and I looked sadly at our broken angel once more. But I noticed something surprising. The tornado had torn off both of her wings, yes, but they were set down gently behind her. Almost as if she'd decided to take them off herself. *Perhaps she doesn't need her wings for now*, I thought. She's just going to stay here with my family for a while. New trees will grow up around her, and our house will be rebuilt. Meanwhile the driveway angel still marks the spot of the woman who has everything because she has the Lord and the love of her children. That's a sanctuary no storm can threaten.

Two Step and Me

GREG ASIMAKOUPOULOS

Ever since he was a little boy playing with his cousins in rural Illinois, Peter dreamed of adventure. He loved to spend hours hiking and swimming and constructing physical competitions to test his endurance. When he entered Wheaton Academy, he jumped at the opportunity to spend his summers going on mission trips. They included evangelistic adventures to Alaska, Arizona, Guatemala, and the Dominican Republic.

Without admitting it to anyone, Peter began to plan to walk the Appalachian Trail the summer after his freshman year at Wheaton College. He talked to one of the leaders from his mission trips for some trusted advice. "He thought it was a great goal, but he didn't think a three-month summer vacation was enough time to do it," Peter says with a smile. "He told me that from everything he'd read, it takes the average person a minimum of six months to complete the Appalachian Trail. But as I continued to press him, he eventually backed off and said I just might be the one who could pull it off."

Peter began a five-month program of cardiovascular

and strength conditioning. In addition to weight training and a daily regimen of calisthenics, Peter came up with his own approach to get his legs in shape. "I crammed my backpack full of textbooks and blankets and then wore it while clocking miles on the StairMaster in the weight room," Peter says. "I got some pretty interesting looks. But I didn't mind. I knew what my goal was." He also talked his friend John into being a human backpack. Carrying his 175-pound classmate piggyback, Peter proceeded to climb the eight floors of his dorm several times a week.

Finally, with his family and church friends praying for his health and safety, Peter waved good-bye to his dad and brother and stepped off at the trailhead in Springer Mountain, Georgia, on May 12, 2002.

By day eight of his adventure, Peter was blindsided by homesickness and blisters on his feet the size of his thumbs. On day nine Peter found a pay phone and called Doug Franklin, who had coordinated the mission trips he had been on in high school. "Doug could hear my voice shaking," Peter says. "He could tell I needed encouragement. He told me a couple things that really buoyed my spirits. First he said that on a long trip you can't just focus on the ultimate destination. Instead, you have to focus on getting through each day. He also said I had to find something every day to make the trek special.

"The Lord knew I needed that shot in the arm," Peter

says. "For the next month I was able to maintain my momentum and keep a positive attitude. Chewing on Psalm 119 every morning and devouring letters from home helped me to keep my focus. But I gotta tell you—although I relied on Snickers bars to give me quick energy, after two hundred of them, they grew pretty sickening!"

On day thirty-eight Peter hit another low. Having logged 213 miles on his second pair of hiking boots in eight days, his feet were covered with open sores. Every step was excruciatingly painful. But once again the Lord knew just what Peter needed. That night at the nearest shelter he met a middle-aged man who expressed concern about Peter's condition. "His name was Rich," Peter recalls. "He told me he used to be a Navy Seal. What was even cooler was the fact that he was a Christian. He spent the next day hiking with me and encouraging me to stick with it. He told me he believed in me."

By the time Peter reached the White Mountains in New Hampshire, he felt like he wasn't making enough progress. When he reached an elaborate wilderness lodge called Mizpah Hut, it seemed part of God's plan. "After being alone for nearly three months, I was beginning to doubt my abilities to keep going. But the Lord knew what I needed, and once again He provided me with the encouragement—and hot shower—I needed."

It was at the wilderness lodge that Peter met up with another nineteen-year-old on the trail. Although his name was Ryan, the boy had adopted "Two Step" as his trail name. Since most of the hikers Peter had met on the trail were retirement age or in their late twenties, he was curious about what had triggered Two Step to tackle the A.T. The story the boy told was more than Peter had bargained for.

"Two Step told me he was only walking the second half of the trail," Peter recalls. "His older brother had hiked the first half the summer before. The brother had hoped to do the second half the next summer but had been tragically killed in a car accident that winter. Two Step was finishing what his brother had wanted to. He was walking to the end of the trail in honor of his brother. That's what his trail name meant."

Peter invited his new friend to hike with him for the final fifteen days of the trek, and Two Step accepted. It was during the last leg of the journey that Peter received news from home that a classmate at Wheaton College had been killed in a car accident.

"It was really a God thing," Peter admits. "Just think of it. Here I am hiking with a guy my age whose brother had died in a car accident six months earlier, and I get word that a friend two doors down on my floor just died the same way. It opened a door for me to talk with Two Step about what it means to have a relationship with Jesus. We talked about heaven and hell and how it's possible to be certain of where you will go when you die."

On August 23, knowing the end was in sight, Peter talked Two Steps into hiking all night by flashlight. When dawn broke the next morning they had gone fifty-two miles in one day and night to reach the base of Mount Katahdin, Maine. There Peter's mom joined them for the final ten miles of the trail up Katahdin.

"I can't really describe all that I was feeling when I reached the end of the trail," Peter says with a grin. "Mostly it was exhaustion. But there was a whole lot more. For one thing I was overwhelmed with how much being a Christian is like a three-month hike. In order to reach the finish line you have to focus on following Jesus a day at a time. I guess maybe that's why they call it 'walking with the Lord.'"

When Dreams Come True at Sixty

CHRISTINE LOUISE HOHLBAUM

It was a rainy day on January 1, 2001. Bustling about the kitchen, Barbara nervously glanced at the clock on the kitchen stove. Only thirty more minutes and the guests would be arriving. At age fifty-nine, Barbara had planned a Beginning of the True Millennium singles' party. As a group of single women, she and her four roommates decided to invite everyone they knew, no matter what age or gender, to celebrate life and new beginnings. With an oven mitt on either hand, she hustled to the door to greet a few early arrivals. In that moment, she had no idea her life was about to change forever.

For eight years, she had been divorced, having ended a third marriage after only a short time. Each time Barbara had begun the relationship with high hopes that it would last forever. After several failed attempts, she wondered if she would ever find the True One with whom to share the rest of her life.

Standing in the doorway of her central Virginia home was a tall, handsome man with a commanding, yet gentle presence. He had arrived with his mother, Lillian, and his sister, Barbara, both of whom were in her church choir. Barbara had known them for years, but had only met Alan a few times. He worked as a prison guard in upstate New York.

The first time she had met him was after a church service several years before, although Barbara had been so distracted about an open house she had needed to attend that she had barely paid attention to what he was saying.

As a local real estate agent, she was aware that he had just bought a house in a neighboring town. At another holiday party his mother had hosted the week before, he had told her he planned to retire there in another three years.

"Are you single and will you come to my party?" Barbara blurted out without thinking how she might sound.

Offering a shy smile, he politely accepted the invitation.

"And yes, I am single," he murmured. "In fact, I've never been married."

In that moment, she wondered why she had never really noticed him before.

It seemed that each time they had managed to connect over the past few years, it had always been a brief interchange. Barbara was constantly rushing about, going from one appointment to another. With a busy real estate office and children now in college, she had spent the last twenty years in a drastic hurry. Greeting Alan in the doorway now was no different. After taking their coats, she quickly excused herself to do the finishing touches for the party.

"Can I do anything to help?" Dressed in a nice sweater and slacks, Alan looked about the kitchen for something to do.

Help? Barbara faltered for a moment. Dangling the oven mitts at her sides, she looked at him for a brief pause. Standing in her kitchen, she thought back to the week before when he had handed her a steaming cup of hot cider.

"Be careful," he had said. "It's rather hot." He had approached her with his hand on the cup, the handle pointed toward her. She had noticed it was indeed very hot, and what a gentleman he was to hand it to her that way.

"Help?" Barbara half-whispered, glancing about the mess she had made on the kitchen counters. What a nice concept! She wasn't anywhere near ready.

"You could lay the fire," she suggested, as she hurried back to the stove.

Sometimes what you want is right before your very eyes. There were plenty of times over the last decade that Barbara would sit in church with hands folded, gaze heavenward and ask, "Please, tell me if I dare trust my heart to a man, again, Lord. Is there a loving, thoughtful, honest man out there who would love me as I love him, someone who shares my values, someone who would go to church with me until the day I die?"

One day, she heard an answer that astounded her. It came swift and sure.

"Yes, and you will meet him in this church. When you are sixty, you will marry him and . . . I have saved the best for last."

This church? Where she had buried her second husband, where her granddaughter had been baptized, where she spent hours upon hours praying for Mr. Right? It seemed hardly possible. Staring out the rain-soaked kitchen window now, she felt a presence behind her.

"Do you have a bucket?" she heard Alan ask. She whirled around to see him with a purposeful look in his eye. A bucket? Barbara rummaged under the laundry sink and came up with what he required. He disappeared around the corner again.

Guests began arriving, and Barbara busied herself with greeting them at the door. After a while, Alan came back to the kitchen for a third time.

"Do you have a garden?" he asked.

Now what in the world? she thought. Then she realized, he had been down on his knees in his party clothes, cleaning out her fireplace that contained four years of ashes and built a roaring fire, a real "rip-snorter" her dad would have said.

A strange feeling came over her.

Her best friend, Kate, and Barbara would often take God trips, the kind of journeys in which only God knows where they would end up.

They trust that their journey will land them exactly where they need to be. On Barbara's fifty-ninth birthday on April 26, 2000, Kate had taken her to a lovely B & B on the beach. They wrote the initials of all their boyfriends, starting with first grade and ending with the initials of their Mr. Right. Not knowing who that might be, Barbara toed the letters A. D. into the sand.

Shortly thereafter, the waves washed away the women's efforts. Kate had Barbara write down all the qualities she wanted in a man. The words came effortlessly. "He listens to me and understands; I do the same for him. He appreciates beauty, truth, humor, different cultures, my children, and me. He loves to play, is generous with his time, his treasure, his thoughts, and feelings. He never thinks I ask too much. He inspires, delights, loves, laughs, plants, builds, is up to making a difference in the world. We build something bigger than the sum of two parts. We enjoy the ocean, Alaska, Ireland, London, Paris, Latvia. We spread joy. He is open to new things, experiences, is sensual, warm, competent, loyal, and FUN! And so am I."

Watching the fire cast a long glow over Alan's face now, Barbara realized his initials were A.D.—Alan Drinkwater. While she remained busy entertaining her guests, she was acutely aware of the man in the ash-covered sweater sitting quietly in front of the fire the whole evening.

Because his mother and sister wished to leave early, Barbara and Alan quickly hugged each other good-bye.

"Thank you for building such a beautiful fire, and please come back." Barbara beamed at him. He didn't return, and she tried to hide her disappointment for the remainder of the party.

The next morning she was back in her real estate office when her secretary boomed down the hall, "Do you know a Native American?" What could she be talking about?

"There's a man on the phone who says he's Mr. Firewater." Now she was really puzzled. When she picked up the phone, Barbara heard laughter.

"What I really said was, 'Tell her it's Mr. Drinkwater, the Firemaker.' Do you like movies?"

"Mr. Firemaker" invited Barbara on her first date of the New Year. After the movie, he asked her what she might be doing in a few weeks when he had some time off. Pretty soon, they were seeing each other regularly. On her sixtieth birthday that spring, Alan took Barbara on a romantic drive through the Shenandoah Valley. She noticed he was a bit nervous. They had known each other for over four months and had spent a great deal of time together despite the distance between Virginia and New York. In fact, he had set a new driving record each time he came to visit.

Saying nothing, he pulled over to a vista overlooking the valley on Skyline Drive. Reaching into his pocket, Alan handed Barbara the most beautiful diamond ring with rows of tiny gems flanking both sides. It was in that moment that she remembered the prophecy she had heard in the church six years prior. When you're sixty you will marry him . . . That fall, they got married at the same church that had been the showplace of so much joy and sorrow in her life. Under a shower of fireworks and Northern lights, the couple celebrated on their horse farm in Central Virginia. Dancing to Barbra Streisand's beautiful song, "I Dreamed of You," Barbara Drinkwater realized now that she was no longer dreaming. It had taken sixty years, but she had found The One. It had required patience and a lot of faith. And yes, he has all the qualities she had asked for.

On the Right Path

JERRY C. DAVIS

Early one cold February morning in 1963, I threw my things into a pair of cardboard suitcases, pulled on my overcoat, and sneaked out of my college dormitory. I took one last look back through the gray Georgia dawn, then scaled a wall and hiked through the woods until I got to the highway, where I managed to hitch a ride with a truck driver.

"Where you headed, son?" he asked.

"Away," I said. I didn't care where, as long as it was far from here.

I'd just been kicked out of school. Again. I was too ashamed to go home to my granddaddy, who had raised me, and 'fess up to yet another disgrace. Another failure. He was a minister, and I could just imagine the kind of sermon he'd give me. *I don't need someone telling me what to do,* I thought. *I can take care of myself.*

I had a friend, Dennis, up in Georgetown, Kentucky. I figured I could crash on his couch. That was three hundred miles away from Georgia, though. The truck driver took me part of the way, then I hitched another ride that left me on a lonely strip of highway near the Kentucky border. Night fell. Shivering, I buttoned my thin overcoat up to my chin. *Lord, all I need is another ride. Is that too much to ask?* I had been taught that prayer was where I should turn in times of trouble. Well, we'd just see about that.

A pair of headlights appeared in the distance. I jumped to my feet and waved my arms. A big rig roared past me in a cloud of dust. *I should have known,* I thought bitterly. *I'm on my own.*

I picked up my suitcases and trudged along the shoulder of the road. By the next evening I reached Lexington, Kentucky. I went to the bus station and spent some of the little money I had on a doughnut and coffee. Then I checked the schedule. A bus left for Georgetown in an hour. If only I had enough left for the ticket!

"Where are you trying to get to?" a man sitting nearby asked.

"Georgetown, Kentucky," I told him.

"You look pretty hungry. How about I buy you a cheeseburger?"

I sized the man up. A stranger offering to help me for nothing? Right. He probably wanted to preach at me, tell me how to run my life.

"Why?" I asked.

"You seem like you could use a hand." I hesitated. The thought of that cheeseburger made my stomach rumble.

"No, thanks," I told the man. "I'm doing fine."

"Okay, son," he said and stood up to go. "Have it your way."

As soon as he was out of sight, I let my head drop into my hands. How was I going to get to Dennis's? I glanced at the pay phone in the corner. I was far from home. But one call to my grandfather and he would help me. *No way*, I told myself. *You're on your own.*

Someone tapped my shoulder. I looked up. It was the man who had just offered to buy me a burger.

"Here you go, kid," he said. "Good luck."

He shoved something into my hand and walked away before I could say a word. It was a ticket to Georgetown.

I climbed onto the bus and fell asleep wondering what possessed that man to help out a guy like me. I didn't wake up until the bus pulled into the Georgetown depot. *I made it*, I thought, squinting out the window. I could just imagine the look on my friend Dennis's face when I showed up at his door.

But at his house, the windows were dark. I rang the bell and pounded on the front door. No answer. Nobody was home.

I felt like collapsing right there on the sidewalk. I was about to say a prayer when I remembered my vow. *You're on your own*. I stuck my suitcases under the porch. I'd come back for them later. Then I started walking, more to warm myself up than anything else. I buried my hands in my pockets and stared through the windows of the houses I passed. Family homes. Tears came to my eyes. I had never felt so alone.

I passed a little church, then came to a plain, nondescript building. A line of men had formed out front. The sign over the door read: The Salvation Army.

I was about to turn away, fast, when a woman stopped me. "Do you need a meal, son?" she asked. She wore some kind of soldier's uniform, yet her expression was soft and gentle, like a mother's.

I opened my mouth to refuse, but the words wouldn't come. I lowered my head. "Yes, ma'am," I said. "I sure do."

Inside, she sat me at a long table with about a dozen guys who seemed down on their luck. Mostly they were older, but younger than they looked, I sensed. Was I staring at my future? Was I destined for their fate? I looked away. Again, I felt the urge to run, to escape. Then came the aroma of food. The meal was nothing fancy—a bowl of soup and a small piece of bread—but it sure tasted good to me. It warmed me and renewed my strength.

"Do you have a place to stay tonight?" the woman in uniform asked me. I shook my head. "Well, you do now."

She led me into a room with a cot. *There's got to be a catch*, I thought. But I was too tired to refuse. She handed me clean sheets, a blanket, and some meal tickets.

"These will get you breakfast in the morning," she said.

I fell into bed. Exhausted as I was, I couldn't fall asleep. Light spilled in from the street through the window grate, casting long shadows on the walls like the bars of a prison cell. That was how I felt—trapped, nowhere to turn. The other night I was alone on a roadside. Tonight I was living on charity. And probably only to be preached at and told what to do in the morning. What options did I have, though? To freeze? Starve? I'd been running . . . from failure, from humiliation. But what was I running toward? Here I was, on my own at last, and all I felt was scared. More scared than I'd ever been. More scared than when my parents split up. My dad was a drinker and a yeller. Mom, a preacher's daughter, ran as far away from her troubles as she could. And now I was running too. I would have frozen by the side of the road if it hadn't been for that truck driver, that man in the bus station, that lady at the Salvation Army.

Granddaddy.

Seems like I always get help at just the right time, I thought. Something clicked, almost as if everything had suddenly been put in focus for my nineteen-year-old eyes. Somebody had to be looking out for me. Somebody who wouldn't let me push him away no matter how hard I tried. In fact, the farther I ran from God, the closer He seemed to pull me.

I slipped out of bed and knelt in a patch of moonlight. "Lord," I prayed, the words finally coming. "Thank you for your patience. Thank you for your love. I don't know what's good for me. Please, I need your guidance."

The next morning I called my granddaddy. I told him about getting kicked out of school. About running away. Everything. Then I asked his advice, and for once I listened. Granddaddy didn't yell. He didn't even tell me to come home. He suggested I stay in Kentucky and get a job, try living on my own. And he said he'd keep praying for me.

I found work at a hospital and enrolled at a nearby college. I finally stopped fighting the world and opened up to it, asking for and accepting help from the people God placed in my path.

That was the beginning of a long road that led to graduate school and a Ph.D. Today I'm still in school, so to speak. I'm the president of a college—the College of the Ozarks. A funny fate for the kid who ran away from school, I know. Or maybe not. Maybe it was where I was headed all along.

Life's Recipes

KIMBERLY RIPLEY

As if I didn't already have enough to do, my grandmother wanted me to drive to her house—two hours away. "I have something very important I want you to have," she'd told me. I was supposed to go to a party that night, and I'd been hoping to get my nails done beforehand. Now I wouldn't have time.

I speculated that Granny might be liquidating her assets, which I knew to be considerable. In addition to cash that was often found stashed between mattresses or in a cookie jar, Grandma also owned valuable antiques and jewelry. I envisioned her handing me her grandmother's priceless brooch or presenting me with the oak armoire that had been in the family since the 1800s. I would have been especially grateful for cash, as my own supply had diminished from a flow to a trickle. It seemed that as much as I worked, my paychecks just couldn't keep up with my expenses. My credit card debt was piling up, and any cash I got seemed to slip through my fingers. My expectations of Granny's gift increased as I got closer to her house.

When I arrived, filled with anticipation of the treasure that was soon to be mine, my grandma led me into the kitchen and handed me an old, rusty recipe box. Its contents were yellowed and musty, and some of the papers crumbled with the lightest touch of my fingertips.

"What am I supposed to do with this?" I asked my grandmother.

"You're supposed to kiss your old grandmother on the cheek and thank her for the lovely gift," she replied.

"But, Granny, it's an ugly green box with recipes—and they smell! You know I hate to cook!" I exclaimed, becoming exasperated.

"I'm sorry you're so disappointed," my grandma replied, looking at me with a mixture of anger and sadness. "Perhaps you'd better go."

After spending mere moments at my grandmother's house, I found myself driving back home. I felt a bit dumbstruck by the whole exchange. I wasn't sure if what I was feeling mirrored the pain in Granny's eyes, or if I was indeed angry that my gift hadn't been of more value. The one true emotion I recognized was disappointment. It always felt like I was setting myself up just to be let down again. I usually blame my parents—they've made so many broken promises to me.

"We'll be back from Rome in time to see your play," they told me when I finally scored the lead. But they didn't come.

"We wouldn't miss your graduation for the world!" Mother had exclaimed when I graduated from Columbia University. But they missed it.

When they promised year after year to come back to the States and spend Christmas with me, but called at the last minute with some far-flung excuse, I simply swallowed the lump in my throat and said, "Sure, I'll be fine."

But I wasn't fine. Now to top it all off I had hurt my grandmother's feelings, when she had been the only constant in my life. But what was Granny thinking? Was this some sign of dementia setting in? She knew my culinary expertise was nonexistent, so why would she give me a box of old recipes?

Returning home, exhausted from the drive, I ran a bath and put the kettle on for tea. After soaking in steamy suds, I curled up on the couch with my tea and my old tabby cat, Lyle. Recapping the day's events, I picked up the recipe box and began thumbing through its contents.

"I remember Granny making Butterscotch Pie," I remarked out loud to Lyle. "When Uncle Ty and Uncle Ben came home from Alaska, she made all their favorites. What a feast!" The cat merely stretched, turned himself around twice, and settled cozily on my lap.

"Pickle Willie and Mustard Pickles! Mother always

made them in the summer, and we brought them to Granny's for the Fourth of July."

I remembered Granny's Golden Chiffon Cake and how she'd make a well in the middle of the flour. That's where she'd pour the oil, egg yolks, and water. She'd always let me stir the batter and lick the spoon.

I could almost smell the sweet aroma of Polka Dots baking in the old wood- and coal-fired stove. Granny would whip the egg whites until they looked like snowy mountain peaks. "Looks like Cole Mountain after a good dusting," she would always say. Then I would carefully place chocolate chips on each tiny mound of fluff. Sometimes my cousins Jo and Lynne were there, too, and the three of us would wait in anticipation for the warm chocolatey treats to be done. After they baked for half an hour, Granny would leave them to cool on the windowsill by the back porch, and she'd always feign surprise when she returned to put them in the cookie jar and found that several had mysteriously disappeared.

I wondered how long it had been since I'd called or written Jo and Lynne. Since I was an only child, they had been like sisters to me. We used to spend weeks on end at Granny's house during summer vacations. How funny to think of them after all this time.

Continuing through the fragile scraps of paper, I found the recipe for the birthday cake Granny had made me every single year I was in grade school.

"Cream Cake!" I cried, startling poor Lyle, who gave up on his nap and slipped off into the bedroom. Cream Cake was a rich yellow cake served with a thick layer of whipped cream for frosting.

My grandmother kept it refrigerated so it was firm and chilled. It was one of my favorite treats as a child.

Granny and I had spent the most magical Christmases together while my parents were away. We'd trim the tree with handmade ornaments and bake spicy molasses cookies. Even that recipe sat before me now in the box on my coffee table.

Suddenly, in the midst of my fond memories, I found myself sobbing uncontrollably. I realized then that my grandmother had known exactly what she was doing when she'd given me the recipe box.

"I've been so selfish!" I cried out loud. "Oh, Granny, I hope you'll forgive me!"

Something my grandmother told me when I was a little girl crept into my thoughts: "If God can forgive our mistakes, then there's no reason the rest of us can't forgive them, too."

How important those words sounded now. Why hadn't I been more understanding with my parents? Daddy's operation had been only days before my graduation, and Mother just didn't dare leave him. And they did send flowers on opening night when their flight was canceled in Rome.

I felt so ashamed. Granny's call had led me to jump to conclusions and assume I would have a newfound financial security. I thought her gift would help free me from my debt and worry and fear. Instead, Granny made me realize that the greatest treasure slipping through my fingers was a relationship with the family I loved. Time and distance had allowed me to grow cold and cynical.

But the recipe box had thawed my heart.

My eyes blurry with tears, I picked up the phone and dialed Granny's number.

"Hello, dear," my grandmother answered.

"Granny, you knew it was me?" I asked.

"Yes, dear. I had a feeling you'd call. We've always been kindred spirits, you and I."

"You're right, Granny," I said, wiping my eyes.

"I think God's reason for giving me a granddaughter was to melt away some of the pain we humans cause each other. I watched and waited while you grew, and I saw you acting like you had it all figured out, though I knew you were troubled. When I saw the path you were taking, I started to get worried."

"Granny, I'm so sorry. I guess I've become so wrapped up in money and material things and success that I've lost sight of what's really important," I confessed.

"You haven't lost sight. You simply lost your way for a little while. I knew the recipe box would rekindle some old, warm feelings," she said.

"But how did you know?" I asked.

"I know you don't like to cook, but the recipes in that box are much more than what they seem. They're bits and pieces of who you are. I thought the memories they evoked might help you reconnect with the past and with the people who are most important to you."

"I kept thinking about Jo and Lynne," I said. "And I remembered some of the things Mother and I did when I was little."

"That box contains a big chunk of your history," Granny continued. "It contains mine and your mother's and now yours. Someday I hope you'll have a precious little child who will grow up having Cream Cake at birthday parties and Pickle Willie on the Fourth of July."

"I hope so, too, Granny," I told her. "I hope so too."

One Good Turn

CHARLES SELLIER

Unlike old dogs, human beings can indeed be taught new tricks. Most of us do change and grow throughout our lives. The challenge, it seems, is to change and grow with purpose; to do it in such a way that we can help make the world or our town or just our neighborhood a little better place.

For most people that just sort of happens as they come in contact with new people, new situations, and new responsibilities. There are some, however, who seem to need a little push in the right direction.

Al and Jackie Miller loved living in the city. They were young, upwardly mobile, as that term is used these days, and black. He was in his early thirties, a successful writer for a small advertising agency and bent on enjoying the fruits of his labor. She was in her late twenties, held a supervisory position with the phone company, and believed that one of the reasons to work hard and get a bigger apartment was to make room for a growing family. In this latter regard Al and Jackie did not see eye to eye.

One warm Saturday afternoon Al and Jackie decided to go apartment hunting. Their discussions about increasing the size of their family always wound up floundering on the shoals of Al's sense of me, my, and mine, so Jackie decided to take another tack. She suggested they look for a bigger apartment in a more "upscale" neighborhood. Al jumped at the idea.

The fact was that Al Miller had made a Maypole out of the first-person personal pronoun, and he spent much of his time just looking for excuses to dance around it. Few of his sentences began with anything other than the letter *I*. To call Al ambitious, impatient, and frankly self-centered would not be far off the mark. Jackie loved him, but she realized, too, that he was becoming a boor.

The Millers had just come out of an apartment house in a neighborhood that wasn't quite up to what Al had decided was his standard, and he was anxious to move uptown. Jackie was scanning the listings in the real-estate section of the paper they had brought with them and wanted to look at a few more apartments in the immediate area. The discussion was still going on when Marsha Givens walked up the crosswalk where Al and Jackie were standing waiting for the light to change and arguing about which direction to go next.

Marsha was a plain woman, probably in her early thirties, and just a little bit preoccupied. In fact Marsha Givens seemed a little bit preoccupied most of the time. A true earth-mother type, she had never married, but she loved children and spent much of her time working with gifted but disadvantaged youngsters from all over the city.

Al didn't know any of this, of course; he just looked up from the paper and saw her start to step into the street in front of a car that had no intention of stopping. In that instant Al Miller made the move that would change his life forever: he leapt forward, grabbed Marsha Givens around the waist, and pulled her back out of the path of the oncoming car.

The driver belatedly saw the woman and slammed on his brakes, screeching to a stop and barely missing the two bags of groceries that Marsha had been carrying when Al's sudden rescue sent them crashing to the ground.

Marsha looked at the car and swallowed hard. Then she turned to look at her benefactor.

"Thanks," she said, her voice quavering slightly, "that was close. I owe you."

"No, that's okay," Al replied. "Sorry about the bags."

The driver of the car glared at the trio standing on the curb, cursed, and drove away as Marsha bent down to try and salvage what she could from her shopping trip.

"Here, let me give you a hand," Jackie said, stooping to pick up a can of corn and what was left of a bag of potatoes.

"Oh, thanks," Marsha replied. "It's my own fault

really. I told them not to use double bags. Why kill another tree, right?"

Al looked on with growing frustration as the two women gathered up what they could in their arms. Jackie saw that there was no way they were going to be able to carry all of the items they could retrieve, so she just started handing things to Al. He glared at her as each new item dropped into his arms but he said nothing.

"Why don't we just help you carry these things?" Jackie volunteered. "You'll never make it by yourself."

"Thanks again," Marsha said. "My apartment's, just across the street."

The two women started across the street as soon as the light changed. Al rolled his eyes toward the heavens, muttering something about not having time for this kind of Boy Scout junk, but he dutifully followed.

"You folks looking for an apartment?" Marsha asked.

"Yes, as a matter of fact we are." Jackie was obviously surprised. "How did you know?"

"Not too many people stand around on the street corner discussing real-estate ads unless they're looking for an apartment."

Jackie laughed. "No sense in being subtle about it, is there?"

They turned down the walkway into Marsha's apartment building, Al reluctantly following with his armload of cans and fresh vegetables.

"This is a great neighborhood," Marsha said. "I hope you find a place. You'd really like it around here."

Just as they reached the main entrance of the building, the door opened and the apartment manager came out. She recognized Marsha immediately and held the door open for them. As they made their way inside, Marsha noticed that the manager was holding an APARTMENT FOR RENT sign in her hand.

"Oh, Joan," she said brightly, "if something's opened up in the building, these people are looking for an apartment."

Al grimaced, but Marsha quickly turned to Jackie and added, "If something has opened up in this building, you really should check it out."

It was quite a scene. Jackie was inside, the real-estate listings jammed into her pocket, her hands full of potatoes, a box of corn flakes under one arm and a roll of paper towels under the other. Joan, the apartment manager, was outside, holding the door open with one hand and clutching the brand-new FOR RENT sign with the other. Al was facing the apartment manager with his arms full of cans and boxes, wondering if maybe he wouldn't have been better off to just let Marsha step in front of that car. And Marsha? Marsha was standing half in, half out of the door, trying her best to match everyone up.

There was a long, awkward silence. Finally Joan

spoke up. "My name is Joan," she said, "the apartment manager. We have a two-bedroom that just became vacant if you'd like to take a look."

"Yes," Jackie said, just barely ahead of Al's "No, I don't think so."

Another awkward silence, during which Al had time to catch the withering look that Jackie fired in his direction.

"Well," he said, "as long as we have to go inside anyway, we might as well take a look." He paused, but nobody moved. "We are going inside, are we not?"

They all laughed—everyone but Al—and went on into the foyer. Up one flight was Marsha's apartment. Once the groceries were stacked on the table everyone felt a little more comfortable, especially the girls. By the time Al added his armload to the pile the three women were chatting away like long-lost friends.

Some might think it's only a slight coincidence that an apartment became available in this particular building the very moment Al and Jackie came along. Nothing could be further from the truth. This pleasant Saturday would hereafter mark a special day in Al Miller's life. He was unaware of it at the time, but this was day one of the miracles that would change his life.

By the end of the month Jackie and Al Miller had not only moved into that building, they were on the same floor as their new "friend," Marsha.

After all was said and done, Al had to admit that it was a very nice apartment, the rent was reasonable, the commute downtown convenient, and the neighborhood as pleasant as Marsha had told them it would be. Jackie was thrilled, too, and even though they didn't often discuss it, Al knew that his wife was mentally redecorating that second bedroom as a nursery.

That, however, was not his biggest problem. His biggest problem was Marsha Givens, now friend, neighbor, and an ever-increasing responsibility. Somehow Marsha, single, a school librarian, and a little bit eccentric, always seemed to be getting herself into trouble. That might not have been so bad except that she always seemed to get in trouble at the very instant Al Miller walked by.

For example, there was the morning last week when Al came walking into the parking lot to find Marsha, a cardboardbox full of canned food in her arms, standing there staring at a flat tire on her old Valiant.

Oh, no, not this time, he thought. He walked straight to his own car, opened the door, and tossed his briefcase inside, but it was too late. He had seen the pleading look in her eyes.

Muttering under his breath, Al tossed his jacket in on top of his briefcase and rolled up his sleeves as he walked over to where Marsha was standing.

"We're having a canned-goods drive at school for

victims of the hurricane," she said apologetically. "This is the last day."

"Uh-huh," Al said. "You got a jack for this heap?"

"Yeah. It's in there somewhere."

Al took the box from her and set it on the ground while she fumbled in her purse for her keys. Twenty minutes later she was on her way and Al was heading back up to his apartment to wash up and change his shirt.

The part that irritated Al as much as anything was the fact that Marsha was such a do-gooder. She recycled everything, volunteered for community service, and even though her own life seemed to be on the very edge of coming unglued, she always had time to help others. This was not the sort of person Al Miller could understand.

"Thanks, that's another one I owe you," Al mimicked her gratitude as he stomped up the stairs. "I should be running a tab on this walking disaster," he muttered to himself. "I'd own this whole building by now."

He was still mumbling under his breath when he came back down and climbed in under the steering wheel of his own car. He looked at his watch, suppressed a swear word, and headed downtown a half hour late. *One of these days*, he vowed, *I'm just going to say no*. Funny part of it was that by the time he got to his office he was feeling pretty good. He couldn't quite put his finger on the reason why, but he felt good. Al was even kind of looking forward to explaining to his boss that he was late because he'd taken time to help a neighbor change a tire.

But that was just one example. At every turn with Marsha it was something new. Al could hardly get through a day, let alone a week, without there being some bit of help she appeared to need. And always it seemed as if Al were the only one there to help. Certainly Marsha didn't plan these things; still, Al had trouble believing it was all spontaneous. Even more confusing was the fact that Marsha never asked for his help. She was just there, in some kind of trouble, and always Al was presented with the same dilemma: ignore the situation, which he was inclined to do, or give her a hand, which is what he always did.

At first he was annoyed, even irritated, by what he felt was a forced generosity. Surely she must see that he didn't enjoy picking up her marbles every day. But as time passed, something changed, and although he would never admit it, that something was Al himself.

One Saturday morning, just as Al was tying the last knot on his jogging shoes, ready to head out the door, Jackie came rushing in.

"Oh, I'm glad I caught you," she said breathlessly. "Marcia's apartment door won't open. She's with her group from the community center and one of them needs to . . . you know . . . make a pit stop."

"Why am I not surprised?" Al said, rolling his eyes toward the ceiling. He shrugged his shoulders as if he were helpless against this continuing tide of good deeds and walked out the door.

Marsha, as I mentioned earlier, was not married. She regarded the group of gifted children she worked with as "her kids," and spent as much time with them as possible. She had "discovered" them, as she liked to tell people, through a reading program she'd set up at the inner-city community center. These kids were not merely bright, they were gifted, and all of them came from broken or otherwise disadvantaged homes. Marsha took these special children under her wing. She provided their curious and amazingly receptive minds with the stimulation and inspiration of museums, concerts, and plays. In many ways she was their best chance, perhaps their only chance, to reach their great potential.

Al made his way through the small throng of eager youngsters and tried the doorknob. It resisted as if it were locked, even though the key was in the slot. Al tried to turn it with the key with the same result. Out of the corner of his eye Al noticed one young girl all but in pain, trying desperately to hold back one of nature's imperatives.

"This might take a minute," he whispered to her. "Why don't you go over there to my apartment?"

The girl sighed audibly and turned around and

dashed for his door. Al smiled and went back to the task at hand.

It took a bit of doing. He had to move the key slowly in and out of the lock, turning the knob back and forth as he did so, but finally there was a click, and the mechanism turned freely.

"I owe you one . . . again," Marsha said, as the kids pushed by him into the apartment.

"Yeah, sure, I know." He turned and started down the stairs. As he reached the bottom step he tossed back, "One of these days, I'm gonna collect." Al had no way of knowing how true that was.

Several days later the Millers were down in the laundry room. While waiting for the machines to finish their work, they were revisiting the same old argument they had had a hundred times before.

"Sometimes I don't think you want to have kids at all," Jackie complained.

"Hey," Al responded idly, "worse things could happen."

"Maybe," Jackie replied, obviously stung by his reply, "but I can't think of a worse thing *not* to happen."

They were interrupted as Joan came down the stairs and headed for one of the dryers.

"Hi, there," she said pleasantly. "Everything working out okay in the apartment?"

"Yes," Jackie said, throwing Al an angry glance, "everything in the apartment is just fine."

Al started to say something but thought better of it. He picked up the laundry basket and placed it firmly next to one of the machines, but when he opened the lid he found it full of somebody else's clothes.

"Oh, I'm sorry," he said, turning to Joan, "are these yours?"

"No"—the apartment manager's shoulders drooped—"they've been there a couple of days. Probably belong to Marsha." She walked over and looked into the machine, adding, "She gets so busy sometimes, she just forgets the clothes are down here." Joan walked back to her own machine and started shoving coins into the slot as if she were angry. "Marsha's a real nice person," she said, on the verge of tears. "It's really too bad."

The tone of her voice and her strange attitude made Jackie suddenly apprehensive.

"Too bad?" she asked. "What do you mean?"

"Oh, it's just that she does so much for everybody else . . . it just makes me mad that she's the one that . . ." Her voice trailed off.

"That she's the one that what?" Jackie prompted.

Joan started the machine and picked up her empty basket. "I thought she might have told you, you seem like such good friends."

"Told us?" Al chimed in, suddenly interested. "Told us what?"

"Cancer! Marsha has pancreatic cancer. It's terminal. And it's a real shame."

Joan walked back up the stairs, leaving Al and Jackie staring at each other in numbed silence.

Later that night in the apartment their mood was still one of somber incredulity. They had gotten so used to seeing Marsha bustling in and out of the apartment carrying boxes and bags or herding some of "her kids," the thought that someday soon she might not be there just didn't want to take hold.

"That news about Marsha," Jackie said as she slipped under the covers, " I just can't get it out of my mind."

"Yeah, me too." Al sat down on the edge of the bed.

"I keep thinking about how at first you didn't want to help her"—Jackie reached over and touched his arm—"but every time you turned around, there she was with another problem."

Al looked down at his hands and shook his head. "And every time I got sucked into fixing it."

"You know what?" Jackie continued. "For all your moaning and groaning and complaining, you like it."

Al flipped out the light and slipped under the covers beside his wife. "No way," he said firmly.

"It's true," Jackie insisted, "—just like the time you ended up driving all those kids from the community center to the zoo when her car broke down. You came home complaining, but you kept talking about the trip and the kids all through supper."

"C'mon. All I said was that the kids had a good time."

"Right. And it took you two hours to tell me that?"

Jackie turned on her side. She could just make out his face in the darkened room. "You know, every time you came back from doing something for her, you came back a little different, a little happier." She slipped an arm across his shoulders and waited for a response.

There was a long pause. Finally Al said, "You're dreaming. Get some sleep."

Jackie snuggled up closer to him. "I love you," she whispered, "I always have. But I want you to know that since we moved in here I'm finding more and more things to love about you."

Things continued on around the apartment house pretty much the same way they always had, over the next several months. Marsha didn't say anything to the Millers about her problem and they didn't think it appropriate to ask. Both Al and Jackie were aware, however, that they were seeing less and less of Marsha. In fact, when it came time for them to leave for a two-week trip to Chicago to visit Jackie's parents, they hadn't seen her for several days.

They were still unloading bags from the trunk of the car on their return from their trip when they noticed Joan standing in the entryway to the parking area with a couple they had never seen before. They were close enough to overhear her conversation.

"I can't get the painters in till next week," she told the man, "but it should be available by the first of the month."

The apartment manager turned and held the door open for the pair as they made their way back inside. Jackie hurried over in time to catch Joan before the door closed behind her.

"Joan?" she said, fearing the worst. "Has somebody moved out?"

The look on Joan's face told her her fears had been realized. "Marsha," she said, fighting back tears, "Marsha died a few days after you left."

Al had come up to join the two women, but he quickly turned away when he felt the tears come to his eyes.

In the silence that followed, a hundred questions thundered through his mind. Why her? Why now? Why so suddenly? What about her kids? It was that last question that really tugged at him. In his most quiet moments Al realized the news of Marsha's death had affected him far more than he could ever have anticipated. And even though he had no way of knowing it at the time, Al Miller's business on this earth with Marsha Givens was far from over.

It was several nights later. The pillow talk in the Miller apartment turned once again to the subject of Marsha Givens.

"I really miss her," Jackie sighed.

Al turned on his side, his face away from her. "Believe it or not," he said, "so do I." There was a long silence and suddenly Al turned over on his back. "Those kids from the community center," he said, "—I wonder what's going to happen to them?"

"I don't know," Jackie replied sleepily. "Maybe somebody will come along."

She drifted off to sleep, but Al was having difficulty putting his thoughts about those kids to rest. At three A.M. he looked at the clock, moaned, and tried once again to get his mind and body to accept the idea of sleep.

Perhaps he had finally drifted off, or maybe he had just succumbed to fatigue and was stranded somewhere between sleep and waking. Wherever he was, he was abruptly aware of a shadow sweeping past the bedroom door into the hallway. Al sat up on the edge of the bed and rubbed his eyes. It was more something he felt than something he saw, and as he stood up to go investigate he realized that whatever was going on was not meant to frighten him.

At the bedroom door he stopped and looked down to the end of the hall. There was nothing there.

This is nuts, he thought to himself, *I've got to get some sleep.*

"There's no time to sleep."

Al spun around and looked at the bed. Jackie was still dead to the world. But he had heard a voice and that voice had said, "There's no time to sleep." He looked back into the hall and there, standing in the half-light afforded by the undraped kitchen window, he saw

Marsha Givens. Instantly he recognized that it had been her voice he had heard.

"Marsha," he stammed. "How . . . ?"

"You've got to come, Al, right now."

Al didn't know what was happening, but he recognized the urgency in her voice and followed after her. When she reached the apartment door Marsha turned once more to make sure he was following, then opened the door and hurried out into the main hallway.

"I've got to be dreaming this," Al muttered to himself, but he followed her nevertheless.

As Al stepped into the hallway he caught one last glimpse of Marsha as she disappeared in a cloud of thick smoke. His eyes stung and he coughed convulsively. This was no dream. The building was on fire.

The image of Marsha faded from his mind as he rushed back into his own bedroom and shook Jackie awake.

"Wha . . ." she stammered, angry at first at his rough treatment.

"Jackie . . . get up! Now! We've got to get out of here."

The acrid smell of smoke hit her nostrils and she jumped up immediately. When they got back to the hallway, Al pointed Jackie toward the stairs and gave her a gentle push.

"Hurry," he said. Jackie realized Al was hanging back and stopped. "Come on!" she cried.

"No," Al said, "for some reason the alarm isn't working. You get down to the first floor and wake up Joan. Call the fire department. I've got to get everybody out of here."

Al turned and dashed down the hallway into the smoke. Jackie could hear him pounding on doors and shouting as she made her way down to Joan's apartment. A few months earlier she would have been stunned at the idea of Al Miller risking his life to save others, but on this night it seemed to her like precisely the thing her husband would do.

By the time the firemen arrived, Al had been successful in waking all the other tenants and getting them out of the building. He was standing next to Jackie, watching the firemen wield their hoses and bring the fire under control, when Joan came up to him.

"I want to thank you," she said. "Helping everybody get out like that probably saved a lot of lives tonight."

Al continued to stare at the building. The experience that had woken him up was now coming back to his mind and the implications of it were staggering. He could almost hear Marsha's voice again. "That's another one I owe you," she would have said. Al smiled. He knew he had just collected the full debt.

"I still don't understand," Joan continued. "What made you get up and go out into the hall? How did you know there was a fire?"

"It's a little hard to explain," Al said quietly, bringing

Jackie into a closer embrace. "Right now I'd just like to make sure everybody from the building is all right."

Jackie put both arms around her husband and held him tightly. The tears that stained her face were not caused by the smoke from the fire.

Things got back to normal very quickly around the apartment building. In spite of all the smoke, Al and Jackie's early warning had alerted the fire department in time to prevent the fire itself from doing a great deal of damage.

Getting back to normal also meant that the apartment manager began to see the kids from the community center going in and out on a regular basis once again. That hadn't happened since Marsha died. It didn't take her long to discover that it was Al Miller who was responsible. When she asked him about it one day he just shrugged and told her he was sure Marsha would have wanted someone to keep the lights turned on for these kids and he always had a little spare time.

Not many months after that Joan noticed something else about the Millers. Al had traded his car in on a minivan so he could get more kids to more places more often. One afternoon, as the van started to pull out of the driveway, the apartment manager saw Jackie rush out, waving and shouting. The group had started to leave without the lunches she had so carefully prepared for them. That, in and of itself, wasn't too surprising, but when she turned to walk back into the building Joan noticed that Mrs. Miller was decidedly pregnant.

Finally, some wondrous power had brought things full circle. One formerly selfish man had been literally forced by circumstance to reach out and help a woman in need, and he had discovered that deep down, it felt good.

Marsha Givens, who could no longer provide the love and attention her deserving special children needed, must have thought that Al Miller was a perfect candidate to take over the job, even if it took a miracle. We suspect she also knew that he sorely needed a lesson in giving and loving.

One final note. In less than a year, little Marsha Miller was born.

Treasure Hunting

CHERYL NORWOOD

"Come on over tomorrow. All the children have gone through Granny's things, and now it's time for the grandkids to come and get what they want."

My uncle had been put in charge of disposing of my grandmother's things since she lived with him the last few years of her life. Granny died from congestive heart failure but had been suffering from Alzheimer's for the past few years. In a way, we lost her months before her tired heart gave up and she went home to be with Jesus. Knowing she was no longer confused and scared but in the peaceful presence of God gave us comfort. Still, we missed her.

Granny had been a mother to seven, grandmother to more than twenty, and I can't even begin to count the great- and great-great-grandkids. We are a diverse bunch, my family. My cousins and I range in ages from eighteen to forty-six. We represent just about every lifestyle out there—from rural country folk to urban yuppies. Managers and executives to blue-collar factory workers. Health-care professionals to secretaries.

Our only common denominator, the glue that kept us connected, was Granny. She loved the biggest rascal and scoundrel among us just as much as the one climbing the corporate ladder. She made us all feel like we were the favorite! She could make us smile and talk and forget our differences and resentments. We'd do anything to see that twinkle in her eye and that face-splitting grin of hers. We counted on her unconditional love. When no one else cared, when no one else wanted us, we knew Granny did.

Granny never preached to us. Her unconditional love spoke volumes about God's unconditional love. In her own quiet way, Granny was our John the Baptist. I suddenly wanted more than anything to find something of hers that would keep her in my heart.

"All right. Is one o'clock okay with you?" I asked my uncle.

"Sure. See you then," he said as he hung up.

Soon I was down in the basement apartment where she had lived, surrounded by boxes and tables piled with her belongings. I wandered from pile to pile, feeling compelled to touch everything, as if somehow I could connect to Granny through the platter she had piled high with biscuits; the pressure cooker she canned with; the blankets from her bed. Had I ever noticed that she liked figurines of little pigs? Was it being a seamstress that had given her such a love of scissors?

As I opened her closet door, I realized that this was

where I got my love of bright colors; every color imaginable jumped out at me from her wardrobe. Red, purple, bright blue. There was the dress she wore to church the weekend she stayed with us. Here was the housedress she liked so much.

On one table were all her treasures, the gifts she had been given over the years. These included mementos and travel trinkets. Although Granny never wandered far from home, her children and grandchildren traveled all over the country—some, even internationally. Granny had traveled through us, been with us in spirit wherever we went. Her prayers followed us everywhere, whether to college or to war.

I was amazed at how much compassion and understanding she had had for so many of her children and grandchildren who had strayed so far from God's best for them. She had been such a good woman herself. Surely God had made her heart, because she loved her lost ones as much as Jesus did. I believe she would have done anything to see some of us not take the paths we had taken. I know she rejoiced when we turned back to God. Either way, she loved us. Even at the end, when she could not put a name to a face, she loved us.

One of my cousins visited her a few weeks before she passed and asked Granny, "Do you know who I am?"

"I can't say your name, but I know I love you," Granny replied.

It was this love that made it so hard to decide what I wanted. There were so many precious items. I wanted to find things that reflected the intangible gifts Granny had given me.

I chose a glass oil lamp. Granny came from humble beginnings, and this lamp had not been bought for decoration. It served a purpose. Granny lived quite a few years without amenities yet had always managed to be joyful. She was a light to her family; this lamp would help me to shine God's light in the lives around me.

I took an old iron, the kind you heat up on the stove. Granny worked hard all her life, without a lot of the advantages and luxuries we enjoy today. Yet she did everything she could for her family. She cooked, sewed, and worked. I think about her hands grasped around the handle of that iron, and the prayers she said for her family as she pressed their clothes and linens. The iron would remind me to keep prayer an everyday part of my life.

Next, there was a pearl-beaded purse with two rows of rhinestones. This one surprised me. Having always known my grandmother as a white-haired, humble woman, this purse reminded me that once upon a time, my grandmother had been young. She had gone to parties; she had danced. She had fallen in love and giggled and agonized over which dress to wear. This purse may have been the finest thing she ever owned. She kept it to remember to stay young at heart and full of dreams. I shall keep it to remind myself that everyone I meet was once young and still has dreams. It will also remind me to keep dreaming myself!

Lastly, I took a little ceramic pitcher from Yellowstone Park. I don't know who gave it to her; I don't really care. It reminds me that all of us were her world. She lived through us and now she lives in us.

No matter where we go, no matter how far, she will always be there. She lives in my love of bright colors; she dances in my uncle's great sense of humor. Her spunk and spirit thrive in Aunt Alice. Uncle Danny and Uncle Alvin look at the world through her soft brown eyes. In each of us, there is a part of her. The same Jesus who lived in her heart lives in ours today. One day we all will be together again. These little earthly treasures remind us of the most important promise, and for that I am forever thankful.

CHAPTER 3

Trusting God in Life's Storms

Even youths grow tired and weary . . . but those who hope in the LORD will renew their strength. They will soar on wings like eagles; they will run and not grow weary, they will walk and not be faint. (Isaiah 40:30–31, NIV)

Batten down the hatches, because life can create some terrifying storms that rock our boats and throw us into the roiling seas. When that happens, we can steady our lives by trusting in our divine Anchor, Jesus Christ. He can walk through the storm and command the winds and waves to "be still." He alone has the power to restore peace and calm in our hearts and minds, if we just put our trust in Him.

Lost and Found

MARY HOLLINGSWORTH

As I entered the church auditorium on that somber Thursday morning in 1981, strains of Elvis singing "Crying in the Chapel" wafted through the air, muffling the sobs of friends and church members. The sweet, sickening fragrance of carnations and various other flowers, combined with the familiar smells of the room where I worshiped regularly assaulted me with reminders that death was present.

Funerals were nothing new to me. My dad—a minister all my life—had not only conducted many funerals, but he had also worked with funeral homes through the years. As a result I had been singing for memorial services since I was in junior high school.

When I was in high school I had even lived in one of the old "house" funeral homes so prominent in the South. You know the kind—a big, stately, white house with a huge wrap-around porch supported by traditional colonial pillars, surrounded by giant oak trees and neatly trimmed hedges. In the one where I lived, the funeral home was downstairs, and I stayed with the funeral director and his wife upstairs for a few months. It's actually a time I remember fondly, because Ray and Nona Murray were two of the happiest people I've ever known. I've often thought it was because they spent their lives serving others and being blessed in return by God.

So funerals and funeral homes didn't bother me usually. But today seemed different somehow. This was the funeral for a ten-year-old boy, rather than an older person who had lived a full life. The death of a child always seems so out of time, upside down, and unfair. And I wondered, *Why would God take the life of a ten-year-old? He still had so much to do, so many reasons to live. What an incredible loss!*

After speaking to several of our church members and friends, I left the auditorium and joined the other singers in a Sunday school classroom where we were to practice the songs we had been asked to sing for the service. Everyone sat quietly, trying to keep their emotions together and prepare their minds and hearts to lend what comfort we could to the family through our singing. As I waited silently for the director to join us, my mind reviewed the previous few days.

Little Justin was on spring break from school; so his dad, Bill, and Bill's friend Tony had taken Justin on a hunting trip in the heavily wooded area outside the city. They had enjoyed a whole day together doing guy stuff—tramping through the woods, shooting at various targets and game, eating a picnic lunch, and then hiking back to where they had left the pickup truck earlier in the day. Justin had been the center of attention and loved every minute of it. It was the kind of day that memories are made of—an unforgettable day.

Bill told us that after lunch the skies had begun to cloud over, and as the day wore on it became first grayer and then progressively darker. The smell of rain filled the air, and the wind was kicking up. So they had picked up their pace to try and get to the truck before the rain started.

By the time the hunters arrived at the truck, a serious storm had developed. Lightening electrified the skies overhead with jagged streaks, and thunder was starting to pop and rumble nearby. Bill and Tony had become concerned about being out in the open in the storm and were moving as fast as they could.

As Bill opened the big cattle gate to the meadow they had crossed to get to the woods, it began to rain in earnest. The three guys hurried through the gate, and Bill told Justin to run on ahead and get into the truck so he wouldn't get soaked by the rain. Meanwhile, Tony stayed to help Bill close and latch the heavy gate.

Following his dad's direction, Justin ran to the pickup, climbed into the front seat, and scooted to the middle of the bench seat so Tony could get in when he came. But just as Bill and Tony turned to run to the pickup, a massive lightening bolt struck the cab of the pickup with a direct hit. The pickup exploded into a giant fireball, knocking Bill and Tony to the ground. Little Justin was killed instantly. He truly never knew what hit him.

Bill was devastated, of course. And he felt guilty for having sent Justin to the truck by himself, even though it was a sound and wise decision at the time. Worse yet, he then had to go home and tell his wife, Joanie, that their precious only son was dead.

Tony was also crushed emotionally. *Surely there was something I could have done,* he moaned to himself. *How could something like this happen? How?*

Joanie had been a faithful member of our church for many years. She came consistently, bringing little Justin to Sunday school and Wednesday night Bible class. She was often involved with the ladies' programs and regularly volunteered to help with events and activities. She seemed to be secure in her faith and strong in her convictions.

Bill, however, had never come to church much. His faith seemed weak, and he refused to get involved in any of the church functions or activities. Once in a while he would show up for a fellowship game night or other fun event, but that was about all. He just didn't seem to have any use for the church.

When the church members became aware of Justin's death, they responded with a great outpouring of love and concern. They did everything they could think of to comfort and console Joanie and Bill and the rest of their family—fixing food, running errands, picking up family at the airport, praying with them, and much more. Joanie accepted their gifts of love and care with gratitude. But Bill, who had never seen or experienced such grace and care before, was overwhelmed by the members' generosity and healing touch.

The next few days went by in an emotional blur for Joanie and Bill. They functioned in a numbed automatic mode, calling family and friends, making funeral arrangements, housing arrangements for incoming family, and trying just to cope with the reality of Justin's loss and the idea of going on without him. My heart broke for them as I watched, feeling helpless to do anything significant.

We made it through the heart-wrenching service somehow, singing the tender songs selected by Joanie, listening to the album of Elvis songs (Justin's favorite), and hearing the words of strength and comfort from the Bible the minister delivered with such gentleness and love. The auditorium was packed with Justin's little church friends and schoolmates, sobbing their hearts out for their lost friend, even though not really grasping the whole situation. It was one of the most difficult funerals I've ever attended.

Over the next few days and weeks, though, the hand of God began to write a surprise ending to this tragedy. Bill began coming to church with Joanie regularly. Sometimes they sat and held hands. Sometimes they cried. But they came. And before long Bill gave his heart and life back to the Lord.

When I asked him what brought him back, he said, "It was the love of the Christians here and seeing the incredible power of God in that storm. I've just never seen anything like either of them before. These people had such true concern for Joanie and me. They weren't faking it either—I could tell. It was the real thing, and it touched me deeply. So how could I ignore the God who prompts people to love like that? I want to learn how to do that for other people, too."

As I hugged Bill and then walked away that day, tears streamed down my face, and I thought, *It's a story of lost and found—little Justin may have been lost to this life, but he has flown into the arms of God, and his dad has been found forever.*

Then I remembered the words to an old hymn: "They will know we are Christians by our love . . . by our love." And I smiled as I wiped the tears from my eyes.

The Fire Next Door

JIM SHERMAN

One night last summer, my neighbor Debbie came over and knocked on my door. "I'm leaving for work, Jim," she said. "Would you mind dropping by my house in a bit and checking on my mother?"

"Not a problem," I said.

I'd lived next door to Debbie and her eighty-four-year-old mother, Nan, for about six months, and we'd become fast friends. Debbie worked the overnight shift at a nursing home. She worried about leaving her mom alone, so she asked if it was okay if she rigged up one of those baby monitors and gave me a receiver. I said, "Sure, why not?"

I was glad to help. But I also felt a little funny about it. After all, what could I do? I've been blind since infancy and out of work for years. In fact, at fifty-four, I'd come to wonder if I had much value anymore. I didn't like having those thoughts and would ask the Lord to help me fight them off. Still, sometimes they got the better of me.

A bit after 9:00 P.M. I grabbed up my cane and headed over to Debbie's. "Evening, Nan," I said, as I felt my way into the living room. Nan didn't answer. Maybe she hadn't heard me. Like me, she was blind—and was also hard of hearing. Quite a pair, the two of us! I made my way toward the sound of her creaking rocking chair. She was cooing to her apricot-colored poodles, Bevo and Biddler. It sounded like they were trying to jump up onto her lap.

"Oh, you get down now, you silly little fools," she said, with a laugh.

Nan and I chatted for a bit. After a while I punched the button on my talking watch: "The time is nine forty-five."

"If you're okay," I said, "I think I'll turn in." Before I left, I made sure the baby monitor was plugged in and working.

"Goodnight, Nan," I said. I picked up my cane and headed out the door.

"See you tomorrow," Nan called behind me, still playing with her dogs.

I locked the door and found my way home. I plunked down into my easy chair, switched on the receiver and laid it on an end table. Checking in on Nan had done me a world of good. "Thank you, Lord," I said, "for giving me a chance to help."

Minutes later I heard a sound—over the years my ears have grown supersensitive. It was Nan on the receiver. She was shuffling across the floor. A door opened. *Maybe she's heading to the bathroom*, I thought. Then I heard something strange, something I couldn't identify. It sounded like *shussss*. Had she turned on the shower? Why? She never showered without Debbie around. Maybe the sound was something else. The gas jet on the stove? God forbid, something catching fire? The monitor was one-way. I couldn't call her. I reached for my cane. I was starting to get worried.

More sounds. A door closed. Tapping sounds, like someone feeling her way around, someone who'd lost her bearings. I got out of my chair.

Then a loud, unmistakable crash!

I headed for the door. "Jim! Jim!" I heard over the monitor. "The house is on fire! Help!"

I went as fast as I could to Debbie's. I had to get Nan out. But how? How big was the fire? And where had it started? I wasn't even sure where Nan was, let alone how I would get to her. One thing I knew: there wasn't much time.

I got to the front door. I could smell smoke, a heavy, thick smell. Now what? *What do I do, Lord? Help me. Help me find Nan!*

I put my hand on the doorknob. It was cool to the touch. I reached for my key and unlocked the door. "Nan!" I called. No sound. Nothing. Was I too late? "Nan, where are you?"

"Here, Jim. Help!" Her voice was weak.

I felt my way inside. I could hear the roar of a fire

from somewhere in the rear of the house. Smoke stung my nose, as if my nostrils were on fire.

"Nan, where are you? Keep talking!"

"Here, Jim, here!" Sounds as if she's right in front of me. I flailed my arms about, hoping to find her. Sweat poured down me. I heard crackling. Not much time left. The fire, wherever it was, was getting closer.

"Nan!" I reached out desperately. My fingers struck something soft. Her shoulder.

"Jim, oh, Jim," she said.

"Let's get out of here!" I shouted. Grabbing her hand, I started to walk and again I felt the panic rise. Could I find the way out? Our lives depended on it. *Lord, you lead us to safety*, I prayed.

I tapped with my cane until we found the front door. We felt our way down the steps, breathing in the sweet, fresh summer air, and to the gate of her yard.

There was no telling how quickly the fire would spread. We hurried down the street toward safety. Finally we had to stop to catch our breath. Did anyone know Nan and Debbie's house was on fire? I heard steps approach. "Are you two okay?" a neighbor asked. "Where's Debbie?"

"She's at work," I said. "Call the fire department. And then call Debbie." Nothing more to do.

"At least we're safe," I said to Nan.

But Nan was in a panic. "The dogs! Jim, where are my dogs?"

"Nan, we can't," I said, my voice now soft. "Going back is too dangerous." Nan began to sob. I understood. Those dogs were more than loving companions to her. They were her eyes and ears. I put my arm around her to comfort her. I can't remember when I felt sadder or more busted up.

We heard wailing sirens and roaring engines and then squealing tires. The fire trucks arrived. Debbie came too. We knew from Debbie's reaction that the house would be a total loss.

We stood around, as if at a wake. Nan and I listened to the sounds of her house coming down. Crackling timbers. Shattering glass. Collapsing beams. Finally, the firefighters got the blaze under control and put it out. But the air was heavy with the dank stench of charred wood and carpeting. I listened to the firemen talk as they put away their equipment. Then another sound. Barking. From Biddler. He ran up and licked Nan's hand. Well, at least Biddler survived the fire. *That's a blessing*, I thought. Soon Debbie, Nan, Biddler, and I went across town to Debbie's sister Dolores's house. There wasn't much to say. Even Biddler was quiet.

Then about an hour later there was a knock at the door. Dolores answered it. I heard a bark, and then toenails tapping across the linoleum. Bevo! A neighbor had found him wandering about a mile from Debbie's house. Nan hugged him like a long-lost child. I breathed a sigh of relief. *Thank you, Lord. We're all safe.*

That's when I heard Nan's voice break. I heard her sobbing, but I wasn't sure why. "Jim, I just want to thank you," she said. "When the fire broke out, I panicked and got turned around. I couldn't find the door. You saved my life."

Now Debbie's voice started to quiver. "You rescued my mom," she said. "You're a hero."

I hardly knew what to say. Two hours earlier I'd wondered whether I really mattered to anyone. And now I'd saved a life. Nan and Debbie were thanking me. Truth was, I wanted to thank them. Nan wasn't the only one who had been saved that day.

Die to Live

HOLLY BAXLEY

Pale moonlight spilled over wispy winter clouds and filtered through branches of ancient live oaks, while a gentle winter breeze fingered its way through gossamer leaves. The effects of this lovely combination made shadowy, skittish patterns on the ground that danced and bobbled below my feet as I walked. Though there was crispness in the air this winter's eve, I took no notice, for I was lost in thought.

Though the night was quiet, in my heart I could still hear the worship leaders crying out to Jesus, and the voices of others that had stood or knelt around me, as they cried out too. It seemed as though there was a holy mantle of awe that encircled the whole meeting room at the retreat conference center. The worship was so deep I found I just couldn't sing. The only sound I could make was a sob, so I just let the tears fall. I cried then and continued to do so as I walked away from the retreat center into the glistening night. The tears kept coming.

A voice seemed to whisper gently in my ears, as if the retreat director was walking right beside me. I could feel him asking me the same question he had posed to all of us earlier that night. "What must die in you that you might live? What do you need to bury tonight when you bury your old life and leave it behind?"

His voice faded as I glanced down fervently at a box I held in one hand. It was just a small, plain, ordinary cardboard box. Though I had been given time during the retreat to decorate it nicely and make it elaborate, I chose not to. Instead, I waited until the last possible minute until a stab of guilt pained my mind. Quickly, I drew a nondescript picture on the lid of the box and wrote my name inside. This box, I was informed, represented my life. And I was admonished not to lose my "life."

And now as I looked at it, I realized what a small pitiful thing it was, for I never took the time to embellish my "life" and make it beautiful. *How ironic*, I thought and walked on.

For I was on a mission now. This wasn't merely a walk to clear my head or to ponder the events that had unfolded during the course of this reflective retreat. No, I was looking for a place to die and bury my old life, leaving it far behind me. For while I held my little box in one hand, in my other hand I held a small trowel—given to me after I had partaken of communion with the other retreat participants and sent outside with a blessing.

And as I looked for this significant spot that I knew the Lord would reveal to me, I began to think about the three questions and answers that were written on three separate sticky notes tucked away inside my drab little box called "life."

What was I willing to give in exchange for my soul?

What was I unwilling to deny myself?

What did I need to die so that I might live?

Honestly, when I wrote the first two questions down, the possible answers really puzzled me. I tried to think of "pious" answers, ones I knew would please the Lord, and yet. . . . I felt no satisfaction in those answers, even though I scribbled them down and placed them in my box. Somehow that seemed to fit who I was as well. Someone who was always looking for the "right" answers instead of the honest ones. Never searching my soul deep enough to find what was really buried at the core of me—answers, which dictated my beliefs and actions.

But now as I walked, it seems as if all the past events that had transpired over my life culminated to this poignant evening, re-surfacing memories that I had tucked away over the years. The radiant spring day of my wedding and the passionate look in my beloved's eyes. The satsifaction of graduating from college. The deep sorrows that flickered in shadows of my heart from the deaths of my mom and dad, both from debilitating diseases—passing away within three years of each other. This same sorrow that increased years later when my husband and I held our newborn baby daughter briefly, before she left this world to be cradled in Jesus's arms. The sweet and incredibly overwhelming memories of awe and ardent love that flowed through me as I held my adopted son and daughter for the first time. And I cherished the new feelings of fervent love with my husband now after a crisis had just hammered our marriage and put it on a very rocky foundation for a while. Right now, life was good. Or was it? Seriously, was I really living? Or was I just getting by on the "right" answers? What was holding me back from loving my husband with abandon? From loving my family the way that Jesus wanted me to love them? What was holding me back in my own life from moving forward into a calling that I knew Jesus had for me? What was this nameless fear that gripped me when I thought about it? I had given it names like rejection, abandonment, disgrace, shame, etc. And yet, they seemed like the "right" answers and never the honest one.

But now on this Saturday night, my little life held a secret written on a yellow sticky note, stuffed in there by obedience and destined to die.

A true answer.

An honest answer.

And honestly, it was so pivotal in discovery that I realized I had inadvertently answered the first two questions by answering the third question with all the honesty in my heart.

And now I was looking for a place for this old life to

die, and be buried. The retreat director had prayed before we went outside that, as we looked, we would see the cross everywhere and in everything. And as I walked, I looked and began to notice things that reflected the cross; on the jungle gym at a playground, in the mortar that crisscrossed the bricks on the retreat dormitories, in branches that twisted gracefully over my head.

And then I looked down and saw where I was to die. There in the woods, by the creek, two trees made shadows that crossed each other. The pattern of the shadows made a cross on the ground. I wasn't sure whether to laugh and think "x marks the spot," or to realize the holy reverence that it took trees to make a cross on the ground just for me. I chose the latter.

I knelt down on the cold ground and immediately felt the emptiness and loneliness of where I was. It was cold and damp, and in the shadow of *this* cross it was also dark and lonely. And I began to cry harder. And as I knelt there on the ground, in my heart I heard again the words that pierced my soul.

What do you need to die, so that you might live?

My hand held the answer. Inside my colorless cardboard box called "life," scrawled on a bright yellow piece of paper were the words: *the need to know.*

The need to know how my marriage will turn out. The need to know if we will survive another season of crisis. The need to know if my children will reject me when they grow up. The need to know if I go forward with the calling God has placed on me, what kind of rejection waits out there for me. The need to know if I matter to God. The need to know if He knows my pain. The need to know what my life is going to look like in the end. The need to know where I am going. The need to know why I've been through what I've been through. The need to know that my heart will not get broken again by future events. The insatiable need to know.

How can I trust Christ, who sometimes does not answer the relentless questions? That when I question Him, I feel the same words in my heart that He once spoke to Simon Peter: "If I want him to remain alive until I return, what is that to you? You must follow me."

How can I follow Him if I cannot trust Him, even when there are no answers? There is no trust, as long as doubt remains. And doubt will always remain for me, if I demand to have my questions answered, if I continue to exchange my soul and refuse to deny my need to know. And what abundant life is there for me, if I continue down this path?

And as I look up at a towering gray tree before me, I have a vision of another woman, also sitting under the shadow of a tree, a piece of fruit in her hand. She too was blinded and seduced by the "need to know," and she chose it over the knowledge that her God knew what was best for her. And she's paid the price for it ever since. And so will I, if I concede.

No, that has to die. I have to die that I might live. And live abundantly.

I grab up my trowel with a fury and start digging in the shadow of the cross. I place my miserable, poorly decorated life in the dirt.

Unfortunately the grave was too shallow. It wasn't deep enough. *Figures*, I think. That's how I've tried to bury things in the past. Just enough so I can say that I've buried it, but always close to the surface so it can be found once again.

Well not this time—I'm burying it for good. I grab the trowel and dig some more. It's still not deep enough. But instead of feeling despair or settling for less, I plunge the steely spade deeper in the rocky dirt, pulling up the deep roots of the common Bermuda grass that clung to the clumps of soil. Determination to die gave me the strength to drive the blade in the ground again, and again, delving out the burial site.

Though it was not six feet under, a proper grave was made. I scooped the dirt and grass back on top of the gravesite. Using the soles of my feet, I pushed the rich loam down with all my might. And as I tamped it down, I thought of the Psalm where King David wondered what man was that God should think of him. David goes on to say, "You made him ruler over the works of your hands; you put everything under his feet" (Psalms 8:6).

And somehow, I realized that this, too, was now under my feet. Buried. Gone.

And as I stepped back to look and make sure it was buried far under the shadow of the cross I heard these words in my heart . . .

"It is finished."

And with joy I walked back to the retreat dormitory, a new creation in Christ. Though it was winter outside, it was spring in my soul. For the old life had passed away. Behold, the new had come.

Pikes Peak Lightning

ZARETTE BEARD

I have always loved Colorado. I was born, raised, and married there before my husband's job took us west. So when the opportunity arose to move to Colorado Springs, we jumped at it. Every day I stood at the window in my baby's room and stared at Pikes Peak. It was a majestic mountain that towered over the city like a silent protector, always there.

I often wondered what secrets that summit held. It looked different depending on the time of day or season. In the winter, the peak wore a gleaming white blanket of snow. In summer, the bald top reminded me that it was too high in elevation for much of anything to grow.

I had chauffeured many out-of-town friends to the top of the peak, much to my delight and their chagrin. The view at the top was breathtaking—and at over 14,000 feet that can be rough, as there isn't much breath in the first place! Their responses were always the same: awe and a bit of fear, especially on the unguarded hairpin curves on the way down. I loved this mountain and would quietly smile to myself as my passengers would gasp and reach for something to hold on to. "Someday," I thought, "I will climb this mountain."

After the birth of my son, I was having a tough time getting back into shape. I would half-heartedly exercise here and there, but with no commitment. I needed motivation. I needed to train for something that would establish a routine and make me be disciplined. Then it dawned on me: The Pikes Peak Ascent race. Every summer, a group of runners and hikers, all of whom are just this side of loony, race 13.5 miles at an 11 percent grade to the top of the mountain. Water stations are few and Army helicopters have to airlift what little water there is on the course. Race competitors encounter gravel, rocks, tree roots and other assorted injurious obstacles. There is even a section in a training manual about encountering mountain lions and the procedures to avoid becoming a meal. The climate at the bottom is drastically different from the top, varying by as much as forty degrees.

This was just the challenge I needed. I could handle these obstacles. *It will be an adventure!* I thought. I could not have dreamed about what lay ahead.

I had decided to practice on the last mile of the race to get my footing. This part of the course is called the "Golden Stairs." Why, I don't know. Stairs imply a walking surface and golden implies smooth—neither of which was true. I found myself climbing over boulders and gripping them tightly so as not to tumble down the mountain and land in downtown Colorado Springs. Perhaps it is so named because it is so close to heaven. After what happened to me, I now believe this name to be quite appropriate.

My husband was patiently waiting for me in the Visitors' Center at the summit. It was a very warm day, and I was running up the trail, about a mile from the top, when a terrible storm blew in. The temperature dropped almost immediately, and I began shivering while sweat beads were still running down my face! No sooner did I begin to hurry up the path than it hit.

Lightning began striking all around me. I was above the tree line, so I was clearly the tallest thing around. There was nothing to get under except boulders with metal in them, so I opted to crouch down in a ball and get as much of me off the ground as possible. I stayed hunkered down in this position while the rain turned to hail and pelted on my back. I couldn't tell which way the storm was moving. I knew it was getting closer to me because the crackling noise that gives warning that the thunder is about to explode in a cacophony of cannon booms disappeared. Now it was just the sound of unexpected gunshots being fired next to my head. I tried to tell myself not to be afraid; it was just noise. But this wasn't the case. I knew that the lightning storms on this peak had killed many people. A section of the top is even called "The Devil's Playground" because lightning has been photographed striking and jumping from rock to rock. Pikes Peak even has the dubious honor of second place for the most lightning strikes in the United States. And there I was, right in the middle of it.

I was terrified. Even with my eyes screwed shut and my face a few inches from the ground, I could see the incredible bright flashes striking around me. I began to prepare my soul to meet my Maker. I already had accepted Christ's sacrifice, yet I found myself asking for His mercy and forgiveness again. I prayed that He would care for my husband and baby because it was just a matter of seconds and inches that separated me from heaven.

Just then, I heard words. I opened my eyes, but no one was there. I closed my eyes and heard them again: "Tell me if you know . . . What is the way to the place where the lightning bolts are dispersed? Do you send the lightning bolts on their way? Do they report to you 'here we are?'" That's right! I remembered the words I had read when a foolish man named Job decided to question the Almighty.

"God controls these bolts of lightening! He can save me!" I exclaimed, and quickly began to pray and ask God to strike around me and to steer the deadly bolts away. I knew I had to get up that mountain to the safety of the Visitors' Center because I was already soaked and, with the low temperatures, hypothermia would set in quickly.

I yelled out, "God, here I go!" and took off running.

I climbed as fast as I could with lightning and thunder chasing me. I made it to the top and into the Center where I was greeted by the patrons' stares as though I were an alien. My husband held me in a tight embrace.

"I thought you were a goner!" he said. He had desperately pleaded for help, but it was too dangerous for the Search and Rescue team to go out.

Gasping for breath, all I managed to whisper to him was, "God controls the lightning bolts!"

I ran the race a week later with a new respect for the awesome power of nature and an even greater respect for the One who controls it. To this day, I take cover when I see lightning and a little smile sneaks across my face. I remember a day when God heard the frightened prayer of an insignificant person on the side of a mountain in a raging storm.

Psalm for the Storm

JEANNE FROIS

I love New Orleans so much I could never imagine leaving. The food, the jazz, the oaks, the sultry summers and cool, bright winters—what could be better? I work at Tulane University, and in my spare time I write magazine articles about my beloved city.

I have written about everything from haunted houses to church ladies' cookbooks to the little pots where I grow herbs outside my apartment window.

I live just a few miles from where I grew up in a shotgun cottage on Joliet Street. Shotgun cottages are long and narrow; the rooms run straight back in a line. Our cottage had crape myrtle trees out front by the porch and a beautiful hardwood floor laid by my mom. Dad hung a swing in the garage door. The only time that swing came down was to bring the car in for a hurricane.

Hurricanes come like clockwork in the South, but I never feared them, not even after Hurricane Betsy hit in 1965. I read Psalm 46 when the winds picked up: "God is our refuge and strength, a very present help in trouble. Therefore we will not fear though the earth should change, though the mountains shake in the heart of the sea [RSV]." *God is truly watching over us*, I thought. And indeed, hurricanes came and went, but that little house on Joliet Street weathered each and every one. How I trusted my psalm.

Last year, when the warning went out about Hurricane Katrina, I packed up my things and evacuated, first to Texas and then to Bordelonville, Louisiana, where Mom was born and raised. *God is our refuge and strength*, I prayed as the storm was approaching. Like everyone else from New Orleans I assumed I'd be driving back into the city a few days later. But I was in Bordelonville for a month. Finally, I returned home on a hot October day. The streets were nearly deserted after all this time. I pulled my car to the curb and shook with sobs. The crepe myrtles were hurled to the ground. Telephone poles were down. The sidewalks where I'd walked with my parents on still summer nights were caked with mud. And the house on Joliet was stained with floodwaters that had risen above the porch—high enough to ruin Mom's lovely hardwood floors.

My own apartment, near a levee that held, was undamaged. I sat in it, staring at the old oak outside my front window. The tree was standing, but some of its branches were down, ripped from the trunk that had supported them. I felt torn and broken too, cut off from the life I knew. I read my psalm and turned on the radio to pass the time. I heard someone say God was punishing New Orleans. *No!* I thought. *God is our refuge and strength.* Over and over I repeated those words to myself. I looked out at my ruined city for some sign that they were true. All I saw was the old oak tree.

Soon after my return I got a call from my boss at Tulane. The department where I worked was relocating temporarily due to flooding throughout the university.

"Can you come in tomorrow?" she asked. "We are determined to get things up and running as soon as possible."

Her voice was strong, hopeful.

"I'll be there," I said.

The next day I drove to our department's temporary location in Metairie, a suburb that fared much better than the city had. My boss was already in the office, looking as crisp and confident as ever. At lunchtime she walked over to my desk, "You know what we need, Jeanne? Some comfort food. We're going to the mall."

Soon we were sitting in the food court with jambalaya and ice cream. I asked her how she had fared in the storm.

"Horribly," she said. "Our house got six feet of water. And my son's in Atlanta. My husband and I are staying with friends in Slidell. We're on a twin bed! I'm exhausted. It takes me two hours just to get to work."

"But you appear so put together," I told her, "so hopeful. I assumed you made out fine."

"We walked through the house a few days ago, Jeanne. It was ruined, just ruined. Furniture overturned, doors off the hinges. I can't describe it. I checked the closets. Clothes were slathered in mud, shoes in tatters, moldy blankets. And yet—I can't explain how—three things were unharmed. My wedding dress, my son's christening gown, and the white communion suit I sewed for him when he was seven. They were pristine."

She fixed me with her strong, calm gaze. "God had His hand on them, Jeanne. When I saw that, I knew we'd make it through this."

We returned to the office and, on a break, I fell to talking with my friends Doreen Barrett and Bea DeLucca. I told them about the christening gown.

"The same kind of thing happened to me," said Bea. "At first my house was drowned, and when the water receded everything molded. I mean everything—except for the angel hanging in my kitchen. All around it there was no damage. That was the only spot in the whole house untouched."

Doreen nodded. "I have a friend who lives in a mobile home. A while back I gave her a fountain with a carved angel. It wasn't very big, maybe a foot and a half tall, but it was beautiful. When my friend evacuated she meant to take the fountain with her, and she set it on her porch railing while she packed her car. But then, in the rush, she left it behind. When she came back she found her whole neighborhood in ruins. But her mobile home was right in its place, the fountain right where she'd left it."

I drove home that day full of thought. All around me was destruction. But in my mind I pictured white christening dresses and winged angels. *Is that you, God?* I asked.

Some time later a friend called me with a magazine story idea. A man was clearing and rebuilding houses for folks free of charge, and every time he began a new project he knelt before the building and said a prayer for its owners. I called him.

"Charles Dillon," he said when he picked up. I introduced myself and told him why I was calling.

"Well, that's very nice of you, ma'am," he said. "But it's not really my story. It's God's story. I was living in Charleston when the news came about your tragedy. All I can say is, before I knew it I was here, doing what needed to be done. I know it looks bad, but I'll tell you something. Everywhere I go I'm finding God. You have to look a little harder. But He's here."

"Yes, Mr. Dillon," I said. "You're proof of that."

By the time we finished talking it was near the end of the day. I sat and looked out my front window at the solid old oak. The tree was thinner with its fallen branches, and I could see through it to the sky beyond. I stared into the deepening twilight and thought about my boss and the angels and Charles Dillon. No matter how hopeless things look at first glance, no matter the sweeping destruction and devastation—the brokenness, the ruin—God is there, ready to refresh our spirit with signs of His presence.

The sun had already set, and I sat in the near dark. The branches outside were black tracings against a serene purple sky. And true to His word, God was my refuge and my strength.

Wake-Up Call

JOSEPH CALDWELL

There were worse things for my family than to have the alarm part of our clock go on the blink, but for me, a seventh grader and an altar boy, the situation was grave. I was trusted to serve every morning at the five-thirty mass at St. Margaret's, two blocks from our house in Milwaukee, Wisconsin. While the rest of my family slept, the alarm woke me at five o'clock sharp. I always got myself to St. Margaret's in plenty of time. But now the means that made my faithful service certain were denied me.

Buying a new clock was not an option. My father was ill and resources were almost nonexistent. There were eight children, five girls and three boys. When one of us asked our mother for something that required a cash outlay, she would respond with absolute accuracy, "If they were selling the king's castle for a penny, I couldn't make a down payment." Suggesting we buy a new clock would have been an exercise in futility.

I went to my mother for some other solution to my

difficulty. Ever practical and well acquainted with common sense, she was ready with an answer: "When you say your prayers tonight, ask God to please have your guardian angel wake you at five o'clock." For mother nothing was more practical than prayer, and there was nothing more sensible than to involve God in one's difficulty. I admit that I had my doubts, but I decided to try.

That night I prayed. I went to sleep. And when I woke up, the clock showed the big hand on 12 and the little hand on five. I got up. I washed, dressed, and combed my hair. I got to St. Margaret's on time, as usual. "Of course you did," my mother said when I returned home.

Will my prayer work again? I wondered that night. I repeated my polite request night after night. My faithful service at St. Margaret's continued uninterrupted. I woke every morning at exactly five o'clock.

Some might attempt a rational explanation. The brain is certainly mysterious, with capabilities beyond our comprehension. It is known that the power of will, given a certain degree of insistence, can invade the farthest reaches and regions of that uncharted labyrinth we call the subconscious.

I have no quarrel with anyone who comes up with a scientific explanation for my "inner alarm clock," especially since I'm probably not the only person on earth given such a gift. But the gift remains with me to this day, and I'm past my allotted three-score years and ten! I still never set an alarm, ever awakened by the soft stirring of my guardian angel's wings. My mother's practicality and common sense never failed her. Or me.

The Best Example

GEOFFREY BODINE

My dad was a man of faith. From him I learned the power of prayer. I pray as soon as I wake up in the morning, if I'm having trouble getting to sleep at night, while I'm sitting at a desk, or behind the wheel of a race-car. Anywhere, anytime. Praying has seen me through the rough patches in life.

One of those was back in August 1994. I was at the starting line for the Brickyard 400. It was just about the biggest race of my career. I was driving against top-name guys like Dale Earnhardt, Jeff Gordon, Ernie Irvan, and my own brother Brett Bodine.

I wanted to beat them all, especially my brother There was some bad blood between us. Like most family feuds, it came out of the best intentions. Mom was sick, and doctors said she needed an operation. Brett and I just couldn't agree about the best way to handle Mom's situation. First, we talked about it. Then we argued. And argued some more. It ended one day when Brett shouted, "I swear, I am never speaking to you again."

"Don't say that. You don't mean it."

"I do. We're not brothers anymore."

"You say that now, but someday we are going to need each other." Brett just turned his back on me and left the room.

I asked God to bring my brother and me back together. Still, I couldn't let go of my anger. An anger that went as deep, it seemed, as my love for Brett. I wouldn't talk to him; I wouldn't apologize or budge. *If this is how he wants it, fine.*

That August day in Indianapolis I was in the lead for twenty-four laps, and ran at the head of the pack until lap one hundred, when I fell behind Brett, into second place. The rest of the cars were bunched up behind us. Going into the third turn, I inadvertently tapped Brett's rear bumper. No big deal; it happens all the time in racing. The bump forced his car high up on the sloping turn. I slipped past to grab the lead. Roaring into the fourth turn, Brett was right on my tail. I felt a jolt. He tapped me! My car went spinning and smacked into the wall. Brett whizzed by, then another car slammed into me. No one got hurt, thank God, but the damage to my vehicle put me out of the race.

I was livid. I shot off my mouth to the press. "Brett spun me out," I said. "We've been having personal problems, and he took it out on the racetrack. I still love him, but he did spin me out."

Our feud went public. Sportswriters talked about the

"battling Bodines" and their "sibling rivalry." Brett said his tapping me was just as unintentional as when I'd tapped him. True, but I was still mad. The one thing I felt bad about was what Dad might think when he read the papers. I had behaved in a way that went against everything he'd taught.

I grew up on my grandfather's farm in Chemung, New York. Grandpa worked the dairy part. Dad and I worked the chicken farm. Side by side with Dad, I learned what it meant to be a caring, decent Christian man. He was always giving, whether it was a meal, a job, or money. People in church and the community counted on him. I can't remember him ever once saying anything bad about anyone, especially family.

In 1950, when I was just a year old, some local stock car racers were looking for a track. My grandfather and dad carved out a dirt track on about twenty acres of cornfield on our land. He built me a micro midget (most folks call them go-carts). One zip around that dirt track at five years old and I was hooked.

"You can race the micro till you're too big for it," Dad said. "After that, though, no racing till you graduate high school." Education first, then racing. The same rule applied to my younger brothers, Brett and Todd. "I don't want you boys getting hurt," he'd say. "We're a family, and we're going to stay that way." As his big brother, I taught Brett everything I knew about driving the micro. But I still wanted to race my own car.

In high school a driver named Pat Justice offered to let me take his car out for a practice lap. I ran it faster than he had, then kept going. In fact, I drove until the car ran out of gas.

Later that summer, our track sponsored a Powder Puff Derby (a race for girls). I borrowed my cousin's late-model car and wore a wig so no one would recognize me. Halfway through the race, I was in the lead. Then I thought about how peeved Dad would be when I got my picture taken in the winner's circle. I pretended something was broken and coasted to the pit. Dad found out anyway.

"We made a deal, Geoff," he said sternly. "You're supposed to be concentrating on school, not racing."

My senior year, I spent every free moment building my own car. I stayed off the track—until graduation day. As soon as the ceremony was over, though, I tossed my cap in the air, tore off my gown, and flew to the Saturday race. I won my heat and placed second in the feature. I was on my way at last.

For two years I raced that dirt track, then jumped to asphalt modified racing in New York, Pennsylvania, and once at Daytona. I met Kathy, a single mom with a son, Matthew, just a few months old. We dated, married, and a year later Barry was born.

There was still one thing missing from my life. "Honey," I told Kathy, "I want to drive Winston Cup." It was the top of the NASCAR circuit. That's where most drivers wanted to be, including Brett, who'd started racing professionally too. We saw each other at the track a lot, and sometimes were in the same race. Seeing Brett's car in my rearview mirror made me feel just like those days when I taught him how to drive.

Dad would come to our races to help sell souvenirs and to cheer us on. He wanted to be close to his boys.

The NASCAR modified division took me all over the East Coast. In 1978, I won 55 out of 74 races I'd entered, a feat that put me in the *Guinness Book of World Records*. We moved to North Carolina, and I drove the Busch circuit (just a notch down from the Winston Cup). I have to admit, the moves and time at the track strained my marriage. But I yearned to make it big.

One Saturday in 1982, I got a call from a race team owner. "Geoff? This is Cliff Stewart. You're looking good. Wanna come drive for me?"

Finally, I made it as a Winston Cup racer. I got named Rookie of the Year. Still, something nagged at me. A question that had been there all along: *Is this why you're really here?* My success had happened in a spiritual vacuum. One day in 1986 I was driving home from Charlotte. As the lush countryside whizzed past, I was struck by vivid memories of my childhood, working with Dad on the farm. Sure, he loved racing. But he loved his wife, he loved his children, and most of all he loved living a life that pleased God. His faith was his foundation.

Please, Lord, I prayed, *teach me how to make you more a part of my life, like Dad.*

A few weeks later I won the big one, the Daytona 500. The next few years on the track saw both Brett and me with some good finishes, some blown engines, and lots more races. I tried to work on my faith as hard as I worked on my driving. In 1993, I heard about a team that was up for sale. Kathy wasn't happy. "Geoff, if you buy that team it will be the end of us."

She said it so matter-of-factly that a cold shock went through me.

"I've seen it happen," she continued. "It'll take too much from us. Look at how much racing takes away already."

But my own team was the next step in my NASCAR career. "I'll hire people to run things," I promised. "It won't be any different than if I just kept on driving."

I didn't seek any advice. Didn't ask Dad or talk with Brett. I just dove in. I ended up with the bitter disappointment of divorce.

Hard on the heels of that, my mom got sick, and Brett and I started our feud. I couldn't imagine how deeply our fighting must have hurt Dad.

Mom got better despite our fighting. Then Dad got sick. That just made things worse. Not until Dad's funeral in December 1996 did I finally get some sense knocked into me. *Couldn't you have given him some peace of mind?* I asked myself. I wanted to do right by God, to do right by Dad and the Christian principles he lived by. When I saw Brett at the funeral parlor, I went over and hugged him.

"I'm so sorry," I said.

For the whole service we sat next to each other in the pew, holding hands and crying. The bad blood dried up.

I kept racing, but now I knew it didn't matter how good a driver I was. There were more important things. Foremost was living a life that Dad would be proud of. *Lord,* I prayed, *you've been with me every step of the way in my career. I know I can never repay you. But I want to serve you more than ever.*

In February 2000 an owner asked if I would drive his Ford pickup in the very first Craftsman Truck race at Daytona. I'd raced trucks before; it wasn't much different from regular cars. I said I would.

Halfway through the race I was running high on the outside with two trucks to my left. One of them got tapped and slid up into me. The impact slammed my truck into the wall with such force I plowed right over another truck. Suddenly I was airborne. In that terrifying instant I knew I was going to die. I couldn't do anything to stop it. I tried to pray, but all that came out was a desperate, wordless plea. All at once, Dad's face was before me. "I'm coming to see you," I said.

"No, Geoff. It's not time. The Lord has more for you to do." Then his face disappeared.

The next thing I remember is being carried on a stretcher to an ambulance. Later, when I saw it on TV, I could hardly believe it. My truck flipped countless times, tearing out 150 feet of fencing. The smoking engine landed on the infield grass. Twelve trucks were involved in the accident, but my wreck was by far the worst. The crowd was silent. When I moved my arm, everyone cheered.

Brett rushed to the hospital. "Everyone's saying there was no way you could have survived," he told me.

I said it wasn't luck or safety restraints that saved me. "It was a miracle, Brett."

People still ask me about the accident. I tell them how terrifying it was. But then I talk about how peaceful I felt when God showed me Dad's face. He'd told me I had more to do. At first I wasn't sure what that meant. Then I prayed about it, and the answer came. Millions of people saw my accident on TV. And I'm here to tell them I'm alive only by the grace and power of God.

So that's what I do. I'm sure Dad would be proud. After all, it's his example that keeps me on track, anywhere, anytime.

Voice in the Valley

NANCY MAGGIO

It wasn't easy keeping up with my older brother, Fred, but I would not let him leave me behind, especially during the two weeks each summer we spent with our grandmother in the San Bernardino mountains. Whatever Fred did—fishing in the stream, horseback riding, swimming, or chasing squirrels in the woods—I was close behind. Early one morning he decided to go for a hike.

"Wait for me," I said kicking off the blankets and jumping out of bed.

Quietly, so as not to wake Grandmother, we slipped outside. The sun was just coming up over the mountains as we started down the trail, our sneakers swishing through the dew-soaked grass.

"Let's take the longer trail," Fred said, pushing his glasses up on his nose. "We'll still be back in time for breakfast." He marched off with me hurrying behind him. I was so busy keeping my eye on my brother I barely noticed how long we'd been hiking until the hot sun on my arms made me look up at the sky.

"I bet Grandmother is awake by now," I said as we arrived at the top of a hill.

"We'd better get back quick," he said. "I don't want cold oatmeal for breakfast!" He surveyed our position. "Let's take a shortcut. We can cut across that valley down there. But let me go first."

Fred started down the steepest side of the hill. "Be careful," I called nervously. *Fred knows what he's doing*, I thought. *He always does*. But partway down the hill Fred stumbled and fell, tumbling faster and faster. I flinched at every stump, log, and rock he hit before landing in a heap at the bottom.

"Are you all right?" I cried, taking a tentative step down the slope.

"Stay where you are," Fred answered through gritted teeth. He gripped his leg like he was in a lot of pain. "It's too steep."

No way, I thought. *Where you go I follow*. I wasn't going to leave him all alone and hurt. *If I'm really careful, I won't fall*, I thought, but sure enough I lost my balance and rolled to the bottom right beside Fred.

"Now I'm really gonna get it," he said. I stood up. Other than a few scrapes, I was okay. Fred blinked up at me from the ground. His glasses were gone, lost somewhere on the hill, and his face looked naked without them.

"Nancy," he whispered. "I think I broke my leg. And I don't know where we are."

Fred was lost? It took a minute for the idea to sink in. How would we get out of here now that my brother was lost, unable to walk, or even to see? I sat down next to him. "We'd better pray," I said. Fred agreed. "God," I said, "please help us get home." I helped Fred to his feet and slipped his arm around my shoulders. We started walking east, one slow step at a time. Then I heard my name, far away, on the breeze.

"What was that?" I asked.

"I don't know," Fred said.

I stood still and listened. "Nancy!" I heard clearly. "Fred!"

"It's Grandmother!" I cried. "She's calling for us. That way!"

"I hear her too," Fred said. He gripped my shoulders tighter, and we quickened our pace. Each time we were unsure of exactly where to go Grandmother would call our names again. "Her voice is getting louder," Fred panted. "We're almost there!"

Finally, our cabin appeared. Fred sat down by a rock, and I ran the last few yards to the door.

"Grandmother! Grandmother!" I called, bursting through the door. "Fred needs a doctor. Quick!" Grandmother came running, still in her nightgown. I told her how we got lost as we hurried to Fred's side. "How did you find your way home?" she asked, bending down to examine his leg.

"We heard you calling us," he said. "We followed your voice."

"But I wasn't calling you," Grandmother said. "I didn't even know you two were gone."

With Fred's leg in a cast for the rest of the summer I had plenty of time to think about that voice in the valley. All my life I had followed my big brother, afraid of being left behind. Now I knew that God would never let that happen. He was always right there with me.

Discovering the Joy of Truth

If you continue to obey my teaching, you are truly my followers. Then you will know the truth, and the truth will make you free." (John 8:31–32, NCV)

Discovering the truth—about ourselves, about others, about life, and about God—is a lifelong pursuit. Sometimes hearing the truth is not easy, and yet, in the long run, it will inevitably free us from fear. This pursuit of truth is one we should undertake with all our hearts, because it's the key to a joyful life.

Pursuing Truth

RON WHEELER

As many of you know, I am a cartoonist by profession. I began drawing cartoons from the moment I could pick up a pencil. However, it wasn't until college that I started to become successful with it. While there, I drew a comic strip called "Ralph" for the school paper. Ralph was a hit with the students because I poked fun at a lot of things with which they could identify. People would tell me that there was a lot of truth in what I wrote. This led me on a long journey to pursue what truth really is, so I could then relate it through my comic strip.

I knew that there was a lot about life I hadn't learned yet. So, I thought that if I experienced all life had to offer, I would understand truth. This zeal for experiencing life enabled me to enjoy many things from mountain climbing to sky diving. I thought I had it all. After graduation, I landed a great job in a major corporation. I had a hot new sports car, and I even had more hair on my head. But there was a lot I was missing too. All that notoriety in college didn't carry over into the real world. I found that spending time trying to experience life wasn't gaining me friends, and I found inner contentment becoming more and more elusive. By this time, my thirst for adventure had led me into immoral areas where I didn't belong.

Fortunately, it wasn't long before I got fired from my job and my life fell apart. I say "fortunately" because if it hadn't, I might not have come to grips with the fact that there is a lot about life, such as inner peace, that I can't experience through my own strength. For the first time, I began to seek help in the church.

I was surprised to learn at church that the Bible had a lot to say to me personally. I learned that God had always loved me, but my pride and selfishness kept me from experiencing that love. I also learned that God already knew about my life of sin and sent His son, Jesus, to pay for my sins through His death. By inviting Christ into my life, I could freely come before the Lord and experience His love.

One night, this finally made sense to me. I was at the end of my rope and had no place else to turn. I had been trying to become a cartoonist in my own strength. My identity was wrapped around my abilities in this area. My pride was such that I actually thought I was a better person than others because I could draw cartoons. However, the more I tried to make it as a cartoonist, the more doors seemed to be slamming in my face. Finally, I let go of my desire to be a cartoonist. In fact, I let go of my very life itself. I just wanted to be right with God. So, I cried out to God and placed my total trust in Jesus.

The irony of all this is that the day after I accepted Christ, I got my first full-time job as a cartoonist and it was waiting for me for three months, right across the street from my apartment. After I gave my life to the Lord, He opened doors so I could be used where He wanted me. You see, He created me with the desire and the ability to be a cartoonist, and He wanted to fulfill His purposes through me. But He couldn't use me until He had me. Once He had me, the doors began flying open for me to be used drawing cartoons as a communication vehicle for spreading God's truths. Now, I am drawing cartoons that are published all over the world. I am fulfilled in that purpose. What is even more satisfying is that God has filled me with His peace for eternity. I had been searching for peace for so many years (I actually thought true peace was an illusion), and now . . . I have it because of the personal loving relationship I have with God through Jesus Christ.

Free to Be

JODY WINTER

I waved from the living-room window as my husband, Pat, backed the car down the driveway, our daughters Hannah and Maggie in the backseat. The girls waved back. Happy. Carefree. Off to their dance lesson. I wanted to go with them. But I couldn't. Maybe not ever again. Not after what had happened the last time.

I stood at the window that Saturday morning long after the car was out of sight, as if I'd waved good-bye to my family forever. I used to play volleyball. I used to be a corporate communications director. I used to bake cookies, paint, take part in my girls' activities. No more. *I'm a prisoner*, I thought, *a prisoner in my own home. All because of epilepsy.*

Epilepsy is a neurological condition in which brief, intense bursts of electrical energy in the brain cause seizures—changes in consciousness, body movements, or senses. In my case, seizures made me thrash, drool, lose control of my bladder, and convulse. The disease had come on suddenly, at age thirty. I tried so many medications, but they didn't help. The debilitating seizures happened more frequently, five or six a day eventually.

My good friend Betty usually came over to keep me company (and to keep an eye on me) when Pat was at work. We had a babysitter come to watch the girls after school. I wanted to take care of them. Desperately. But it was hard enough just taking care of myself. No driving; my neurologist wouldn't approve me for a license renewal. I couldn't even risk leaving the house without another adult. Not that I wanted to. The seizures were bad, but the humiliation was worse. One minute I'd be putting groceries into a cart, and the next I'd be laid out on the supermarket floor, wiping drool from my mouth, and staring up at panicked faces.

The last time I'd gone to the girls' dance class I sat in the back of the studio. I was trying to keep myself calm, quiet. Suddenly I had a seizure. Seconds later I came out of it, but it could have been hours for all I knew. I looked up from the floor at the horrified stares of the little girls. *Never again*, I promised myself. *I don't want Hannah and Maggie getting teased about their mom, the epileptic.*

I went home and stayed there. Pat went to work and the girls went to school. I'd wake up, have a seizure, fall asleep. Over and over, day after day, one blurring into the next, too afraid to go out in public for any reason.

When Pat and the girls got back that afternoon, Hannah announced, "Mommy, look what I learned today!" She showed me a new step. "I wish you had come with us."

So did I. But it was just a wish, a sad, hopeless wish. I was not going to get better. Not through doctors. Not through the love of my family. Not even through prayer. I'd given up on that too, I suppose.

"You've been cooped up in the house too long," Pat said to me one Sunday morning. "You need to come to church with me and the girls." Before I could protest he said, "It's the one place you're not going to be judged."

We'll see, I thought.

We dropped the girls off at Sunday school, then slipped into the sanctuary. I insisted on sitting in the back row. I stared at the bulletin rather than risk making eye contact with someone I knew. I felt angry, angry at what I'd become. *God, why has this happened to me?*

An announcement in the bulletin caught my eye: "Children's Christmas program volunteers needed—sets, programs, costumes." Right up my alley. At one time, anyway. I thrust my finger at it and said to Pat after the service, "I wish I could do something like this again!"

"So, why not try?" he answered.

Why not? I could give five or six reasons a day why not.

Still, Pat's question rang in my head: *why not try?* Hadn't I been trying? Yet something told me that if I gave up on this, I might as well give up for good. So a few nights later I had Pat drop me off for the Christmas program meeting. Eight other women came. "I was in marketing and design before I had epilepsy," I said when it was my turn to introduce myself.

"We could use you," said one woman. "None of us is very creative. You should be our chair."

"I can't," I insisted. "I don't have the strength to do it because of my seizures. It's impossible."

"Impossible?" another woman chimed in. "Impossible is one of us ever designing anything. You're it, seizures or no seizures."

And that was that. But I couldn't help worrying that I might end up disappointing them.

I set up a meeting with the family ministry pastor and his youth coordinators a couple of days later. We were to discuss budget needs and schedules. But first they wanted to go over the script. Fine. I handed out the outlines. The next thing I knew, I was coming to, on the floor. Oh, no . . . How bad of a seizure was it? Would they put someone else in charge? "Give me a second to pull my dignity out of my pocket," I joked.

The pastor helped me sit up. "We're thankful you're willing to take charge of the show," he said. "It's incredibly brave of you. You must have quite a faith."

I wondered at the pastor's words. Quite a faith? If he only knew.

I wasn't replaced, though we did come up with a backup plan so others could step in to run things, if necessary.

It was only after I left the pastor's office that I thought of his reaction to my seizure. Or lack of reaction, to be exact. *You flopped around and he didn't even question it*, I thought. It was no big deal to him. Did it have to be such a big deal to me? I'd asked God for healing, expecting it. Maybe what I needed was acceptance.

I prayed hard before the first Christmas program rehearsal. It took a lot of courage to tell three hundred children about my epilepsy. "Sometimes my body goes crazy," I explained. "But it's nothing to be afraid of. After a little bit, it stops. And then I'm fine." The kids seemed to think nothing of it, even after I had a seizure in front of them.

I couldn't understand it at first. But as the weeks went by I realized the kids saw me as a person, not as an epileptic. Could I, too, see myself as a person? The fear I'd lived with for so long faded. In its place I felt a glow, the warm glow of acceptance. *This is how it's going to be*, I decided. *I don't understand it. I can't change it. But I won't let it stop me from living the life God's given me. I don't have to be afraid.*

The church was packed for the Christmas show. It was a major hit. I was back in the saddle.

With time, and adjustments in medication, my seizures came less frequently. Five or six a week, not a day. Still, I couldn't drive or go out alone. "Never leaving the house on my own gets so old," I complained to my friend Betty. "I need a girls' night out."

"So do I," she said. "I've got two teenagers at home who are driving me up a wall."

"What should we do?" I asked.

"We could rent a van and take a day trip," Betty said.

"I can't drive," I reminded her. "That wouldn't be fair to you."

"Maybe we could rent one of those shuttle vans with a driver."

We went to check out rentals one Saturday. The company owner, Tim, showed us a really nice van. "If you think that's something, take a look at this," he said, leading us to a full-size tour bus. Wow. Plush, comfy seats and legroom galore.

"Awesome," I said. "If only we had fifty friends to fill it!"

"Why not?" Betty said.

Why not? That question had come up before, hadn't it?

We rented the bus and signed up fifty-two women for an overnight tour around Minnesota—a luncheon cruise, an evening at a comedy club, and tons of surprises. We had a blast, the best time some of us had had in years.

The next day one of the women called me up. “Promise me we’ll do that again,” she insisted.

So I arranged another trip. There was so much interest that I added two more tours. That winter it was five. I’m still at it today. I call my business “Girls Fun Adventures.” And, despite epilepsy, and thanks to God and my family, that’s what my life has become: an adventure in living.

So You Think You're a Stud!

NORRIS BURKES

During my days of service as an Air Force chaplain, I enjoyed a lot of titles. Navy folks called me "Chappy." British colleagues called me "Padre." A Vietnam vet I knew even used to call me "Sky Pilot" after the 1968 Eric Burdon song.

However, none of those names compare to what I was once called at our hospital senior center. Walking into the center to lead an afternoon Bible study, the recreation director keyed the microphone to make her usual announcement: "We are now ready for our Bible study." But this time, a slip of the tongue caused a slight variation in her last word, adding a huge difference to its meaning. With the omission of the last letter, she inadvertently prepped this audience of one hundred seniors for the appearance of the "Bible stud."

Studs are usually tough guys and, while everyone was playfully amused with my new title, they knew I wasn't really so tough. In fact, none of us is ever the tough "stud" we imagine ourselves to be. Toughness can be a costume we don from our own weak need to be somebody we're not. We've all put on the tough-guy act or met someone auditioning for the part, but I had one particular late-night meeting with a tough guy I'll never forget.

The meeting took place on a darkened street just outside the chapel where I was serving as an active duty chaplain in Izmir, Turkey. The players involved included myself and an army sergeant who was playing the tough-guy, stud role with his wife and children. From just beyond the exposure of streetlights, I heard his wife demanding to be released. While his answer would cause some to blush, it made me flush—with anger. Evidently he was one of those men who thought being a stud meant making "the woman" do what she was told.

Imagining myself to be a bit of a stud myself, I stepped toe-to-toe with the sergeant and initiated some point-blank introduction in the melodramatic style of an old *Dragnet* episode.

"I'm Chaplain Burkes," I asserted, offering my ID card. "May I see your ID please?"

In the next few moments we mutually examined IDs as if we were putting a poker hand on a table, but the sergeant quickly folded to my better hand as a captain—a straight beats a pair of jacks.

"Let her go, Sergeant!"

He let her go but grabbed the children in trade. "She can go, but the children go with me!"

"Let them go, Sergeant!" I ordered with a syllabic staccato. "That's an order—a direct order!"

If your military knowledge is limited to *Hogan's Heroes*, you might think captains are always barking, "That's an order!" But actually the suffix is very rare for any order. In fact, in sixteen years with the military, this had been the only time I'd ever said it, but it worked. He let them go. I told him that I would escort his wife and children home, and I ordered him to separate quarters.

"Sergeant, you will report to my office by noon tomorrow," I told him. "If you don't show, I'll bring this show to your commander's office. If you do show, I can promise you complete confidentiality in our counseling." This promise was true to military guidelines that gave every person I counseled complete confidentiality. Even if someone were to confess a murder or a treasonous act, a chaplain cannot reveal that to anybody. But, like any other officer, if I personally observed a wrongful act, as I had done that night, I could report that to his commander.

He knew that, which was mostly why he made the appointment the next day. Emboldened by the confidential sanctuary of the chaplain's office, they both came into my office screaming and threatening each other with divorce and child custody battles. Things quickly became so venomous that future counseling appointments were scheduled separately. But, over the next several days the husband finally began talking about what toughness meant with his "old man" and about the toughness the army had taught him, which he had transferred to his home life.

Somewhere in all of that, a miracle broke through. This tough stud finally broke down and admitted he wasn't so tough after all. He spoke of sitting in his fifth-floor apartment window night after night wanting to jump. He spoke of a presence that held him in that window and would not let him jump. He talked of his failing family life and career.

He told me his family needed a miracle. "Is there any hope?" he asked. I told him it all depended on his willingness to redefine and transform what it meant to be a "tough stud." He said he was willing. Eventually, the husband and wife began to rebuild their love for each other and to their Creator. They took classes in anger management and sought the support of a faith community.

They pledged a new commitment to the biblical admonition to "submit themselves one to another in fear of God." Not one submitting to the other, as he had demanded she do, but submitting equally, one toward the other.

Sometime later that year, as I prepared for my return to the United States, I found them to say my good-byes. "Chaplain," she said, "I think when you look at us now, you'd have to say you were looking at a miracle." I smiled at the understatement.

Then I noticed another miracle. She must have caught the question in my eyes. "Yup, I'm pregnant," she said, beaming. "And I made promotion," he added as the miracles continued.

Besides the obvious meaning for stud, "kept for breeding," the dictionary gives another meaning—"a straightening crosspiece." I'd never seen someone become such a stud as fast as I did the day I saw this husband weeping before his wife and His Creator in search of forgiveness. His admission of weakness miraculously became the stud—the strengthening crosspiece—of a new relationship. Perhaps using this definition, there is a way to be a stud after all.

Waffle House Waitress

JOSEPH MCCORD

My theme song could have been "On the Road Again" when I worked for an insurance company in Spokane. I drove all over Washington State, meeting with agents and execs. Each trip blurred into another—the contracts, the dinners, closing the deal. Same old, same old—except one trip I'll never forget.

I had business in Seattle, an easy drive about 300 miles west, but I planned to stay overnight with friends along the way. I was looking forward to it. They lived on the northwestern edge of the Colville Indian Reservation.

Driving was second nature, as I said, but I couldn't shake a foreboding feeling, almost from the time I got behind the wheel. It was hard to describe, like I was headed into some kind of danger. Ignored it was what I did. Or tried to. Once under way, I would have said a quick prayer to my guardian angel, if I believed stuff like that. But I didn't, absolutely. I didn't believe in messages from beyond, or things that go bump in the night. I was a rational guy. I concentrated on the mountains and plains. Beautiful country. Then I saw black clouds up ahead. A storm. I'd driven in storms before. My car was in tip-top shape. But those clouds were as dark and scary as my mood. Why did I feel like disaster waited for me out there? The farther west I drove, the stronger the feeling became.

Eventually I took the highway north toward the reservation. The weather only got worse. I gripped the wheel tight. After a while I was shaking. I couldn't keep driving. "Take a break," I told myself. It was the sensible thing to do. A cup of coffee would surely set me straight. Treacherous mountain roads lay ahead. I had to have my wits about me.

I spotted the neon sign of a Waffle House. *Perfect.* I pulled into the parking lot and went inside. A waitress came up to the counter. "Coffee," I said. "Black."

"Are you all right?" she said. "You look like you've seen a ghost."

I didn't believe in ghosts, but I said, "Well, maybe I did." *Maybe my own.*

She poured my coffee and left me alone to drink it. I did my best to relax. *What was going on with me?*

The waitress came back to top off my cup. "What you need is a piece of pie," she said. "It's fresh-baked. Apple." I shook, my head. "I insist," she said. "Trust me. You need this."

I was startled to see a glow of light around the waitress.

Like a halo or something. Probably the neon sign outside reflecting in the mirror behind her. "So? What do you say?" I gave in. "Good," she said. "I'll heat it up."

I checked my watch. I should get back on the road. I'd lost time. It was already dark out, and I still had a long way to go. Soon the waitress came back with a piece of apple pie, a scoop of ice cream melting beside it. "Ice cream too?" I protested.

"Eat it," she insisted. "It's good for what ails you." The waitress dropped my bill on the counter. The light around her glowed more brightly.

The pie tasted delicious. I ate slowly, but even that didn't account for how long it took me to get down to the last bite. I put it in my mouth wondering if I'd ever in my life have a slice of pie to top this one. Probably not. And the waitress was one hundred percent right. That pie was good for what ailed me—whatever it was, it was gone. I felt like myself again.

I left my money on the counter and got up to leave. "You drive carefully now," the waitress called.

The door jingled as I stepped out into the lot. I jumped into my car and headed into the Indian reservation.

The storm had passed over. I picked up speed. My friends were expecting me. I zoomed downhill around a curve. What's that? Through the darkness I saw something in the road. Cows. Maybe a dozen cows. The

Indians' cattle roamed free. My lane was clear, but a huge bull was moving into it. Whoa! I was going way too fast to stop now.

I floorboarded the gas pedal and flew by the bull. I missed him only by inches. I could almost feel the breath from his nostrils as I whizzed by. I slowed down a little, glancing to my right. Hundreds of cows drifted across the plain. The entire herd! They must have completely blocked the road for a good while. If I'd come around that downhill curve while they were moseying across, I would have crashed into them. If I hadn't stopped for coffee—and lingered over that apple pie—I could have been killed.

About a month later I was on another trip covering the same area. I stopped at the Waffle House, mainly to thank the waitress. She wasn't there. The manager looked puzzled when I inquired about her. "I know exactly who you mean," he said. "She only worked for a few hours that one day, and then she quit. I asked why, and she said, 'My work here is completed.'"

What's a rational guy like me supposed to think? A temporary waitress and a slice of apple pie changed everything for me. It happened. It's true. I guess you don't necessarily have to ask God for a guardian angel to get one anyway.

The Gift

VICKY TAPP

But each has a particular gift from God, one having one kind and another a different kind.
—1 CORINTHIANS 7:7, NRSV

When the long-awaited day of our wedding had finally come and gone, my husband and I spent many hours settling into our new home and finding the right place for each gift we had received. No matter how hard I tried, however, there was one item I simply couldn't bring myself to use: a wool nightgown in the most outrageous plaid I had ever seen.

Mrs. Sanders was an elderly neighbor; she had given me the nightgown at my bridal shower. When she presented it to me, it was difficult to hide my reaction, and it remained in its box on a shelf in our closet.

One morning as I was hanging out the laundry, Mrs. Sanders stopped beside my fence while she was taking her daily walk. She inquired about the nightgown, asking why it was that, as often as she had passed by our yard, she'd yet to see it hanging on the clothesline with our other things.

I was dumbfounded, not knowing how to respond. In a moment of desperation, I lied to her and said that I wouldn't dream of hanging a gown as unique as that one on the line for fear it would snag and be ruined. My hasty reply seemed to pacify her. She nodded and smiled as she started on her way again. But then she looked back over her shoulder, and to my horror, she said, "Mind the moths don't get it, my dear."

She knew! She knew I hadn't worn it. She knew that I had lied. Knowing I'd hurt her left a terrible guilty feeling in my heart.

Later that night as I lay in bed, I replayed the incident in my mind. That's when I realized I was guilty of a much worse offense than hurting the feelings of a well-meaning friend. Hers was not the only gift I had received that I was hiding for fear of embarrassment. When I gave my life to the Lord, he blessed me with the ability to write Christian poetry. I had been exercising this gift for many years and had a shelf full of my work to attest to this, but I hadn't had the courage to seek publication for any of it. The messages contained in those poems sat under a layer of dust where they could benefit no one.

The audacity of this brought me out of bed and onto

my knees! Who did I think I was that I could take a gift given to me by my blessed Savior and refuse to do with it what I knew he intended? When I finished praying for forgiveness, I remember thinking that the Lord should take this talent away from me and give it to someone who wouldn't let fear stand in the way of delivering his messages.

It was at that moment I felt the Lord's presence. Speaking to my heart in a voice that was nearly audible, I heard, *Vicky, there are others I might have blessed with this gift, but I chose you.*

Yes, Lord, you did. After deciding to never again deny the Lord any part of myself, I arose with a much lighter heart. I slid back under the covers and snuggled down to sleep . . . warm and cozy in my wool plaid nightgown.

When All Else Fails

GLYNNIS WHITWER

With five kids, we didn't go through flu season unscathed. One after another came down with some strain of the flu . . . headaches, slight fevers, and upset stomachs. Nothing major, just a day or two of bed rest, missed school, and Mom's doting attendance. The only child seemingly unaffected was Robbie, our ten-year-old son.

That didn't last long. When someone nudged me on the shoulder at midnight, I wasn't surprised to see a pained Robbie standing next to my bed.

"Mom, I feel sick," he said. His pinched face and arms wrapped gingerly around his stomach told me all I needed to know. I immediately shifted into nurse mode, jumped out of bed, and escorted my little charge to the bathroom, where we spent most of the remainder of the morning. His little stomach rebelled at every sip of water. That same raw tummy rejected each dose of children's medicine Robbie took to bring down his fever. As the hours passed, the fever rose at an alarming rate.

Although the other kids had suffered some, Robbie seemed to get the worst of it. Throughout the day, I hovered over him, wringing out wet cloths to put on his forehead and trying to cool his simmering body. Keeping a bucket handy, I measured small sips of ginger ale and water. Most didn't stay down. After cleaning up, we started over again. This active, healthy boy was reduced to a pitiful, curled up ball of misery.

As the day wore on, his fever seemed resistant to the over-the-counter medicine I'd been trying. As it rose in degrees to 101, then 102, and settled on 103, I started to worry. I searched the Internet for information on when to call a doctor or rush him to the emergency room. A reputable site said that anything over 104 degrees was cause for worry. We were close to that and as the minutes slipped away, Robbie's fever rose to a distressing 103.6 degrees.

I increased my efforts to cool him down with sponge baths and took his temperature every five minutes. My husband was out of town, and I mentally rehearsed what I would do with the other four kids while I ran to the emergency room. *Should I put my mom or neighbor on alert? Should I go now? Should I call the doctor?*

In the early evening, I gathered my fifth grade son on my lap, and rocked him like a baby. Although alert, Robbie was miserable. His thin body felt like a heating pad everywhere he touched my body. As he lay limp in my arms, helplessness and insecurity washed over me. Normally confident, I didn't know what to do. I wished I'd called the doctor earlier in the day, but then it seemed like a normal case of the flu. I mentally kicked myself for not doing something more.

As I sat on the couch, cradling my feverish boy, I heard a voice so small I almost missed it. *You haven't done everything . . . You haven't asked Me for help.*

I knew that voice, and answered with surprise. *I didn't? Are You sure, God?*

Then I did a mental review of the day: Medicine . . . check! Cool water . . . check! Fluids . . . check! God? Hmmm. I couldn't remember saying a prayer. Maybe God was right.

I mentally kicked myself. How could I, someone who prays regularly about other things, have had a sick child all day and not once had I thought to pray to the One who could actually help? Maybe subconsciously I didn't want to "bother" God with something relatively minor. Or maybe because it seemed like a common ailment, I believed I could take care of it. I'm not sure why I didn't ask God for help, but it sure was a mistake.

With desperation, and not a little panic, I thought, *If I'm going to pray, it better be good.* So with one arm wrapped around a wilting Robbie, and my free hand placed on his head, I prayed out loud: "*Dear heavenly*

Father, I ask, in the name of Jesus, for You to please bring Robbie's fever down to normal, and please keep it normal throughout the night. In the name of Jesus I pray, Amen." I wanted to get Jesus's name in there a few times for good measure.

Robbie still burned in my arms. I guess I was hoping for an instantaneous healing. After all, Robbie was four-tenths of a degree from heading to the emergency room. If God was going to act, I was eager for it to be fast. Of course, I conveniently overlooked the fact that I had waited until the last minute to pray.

I kissed Robbie's forehead and soothed his cheek. Even though his fever was still hovering close to 104°, I experienced relief from the fear I'd felt only minutes earlier. Even if nothing happened, at least I didn't feel alone. I gave Robbie another dose of medicine and held him close.

The minutes ticked by and Robbie drifted into sleep. I was so annoyed at myself for not praying that I tried to make up for it by continuing to pray, only silently this time. I thanked God for His presence, His concern, and His power to heal my sick child. I thanked Him for calming my heart and allowing Robbie to sleep.

It didn't take long for me to feel a change in Robbie. As his body experienced its first restful sleep all day, I was certain he didn't feel quite as hot. *It must be my imagination*, I reasoned. Not wanting to disturb my sleeping boy, I sat there for a few more minutes. After ten minutes I couldn't stand it any more, carefully rearranged Robbie and went to find the thermometer. Carefully tucking it under his armpit, I watched in amazement as it read 101 degrees, which actually meant it had dropped to 102 degrees. Ten minutes later I took it again, only to find that it had dropped to 100 degrees. After thirty minutes, Robbie was awake, and I tucked the thermometer under his tongue. Instead of shooting up like a rocket, the numbers on the digital thermometer climbed slowly and stopped at 98.6 degrees.

Normal! How could it be? Only a half hour earlier I was ready to take my son to the emergency room. His fever had climbed unrestrained all day and rejected my feeble attempt to bring it down. Now, although he was tired, Robbie felt pretty good. We made up a makeshift bed in my room, and he slept peacefully and fever free through the night. Robbie woke the next morning with a tender tummy, but feeling much better.

That night I knew we'd experienced some divine intervention. As most moms know, a fever *that* high doesn't drop *that* fast on medicine alone. In spite of my ignoring Him all day, God still answered my prayers.

God's act of kindness and compassion in healing my son has changed my attitude about everyday sickness. I'm determined to not replay that day of ignoring God.

Now, instead of starting my health-care regimen with what I know, I turn to Who I know. I've learned that no problem is too small to pray about, and that every situation is an opportunity for God to work a miracle when we pray. Like the night He brought my son's temperature down from 103.6 degrees to normal in thirty minutes.

Botta Bing, Botta Boom—the Sound of Miracles

TIM BETE

When our daughter Anna Maria was born, she slept a lot—except when we wanted her to sleep. She would sleep in my arms. She would sleep in a car seat. But if we put her in her bassinet, her eyes popped open wide as if she had just seen a gallon of milk or a shiny new pacifier. I should have remembered from my high school French class that the literal translation of *bassinet* is "sleepless parent." *Je suis un bassinett.*

My first night of sleeplessness wasn't too difficult. But after a week I was delirious, and I don't mean in the happy sense. I considered signing up as a subject in a sleep deprivation experiment just to get some rest.

I kept a journal during our first week with Annie at home.

Day 1—Yawning: Only two hours of sleep but I'm so happy about the new addition to our family that it hasn't fazed me. Drank two cups of coffee to take the edge off my sleepiness. Watched three infomercials at 2 A.M. while rocking Annie to sleep. Resisted the temptation to buy a Chia Pet in the shape of Jay Leno's head. Decided I would try to take a nap tomorrow.

Day 2—Groggy: The daytime nap didn't materialize. Used twice as much coffee in the coffeemaker and cut the amount of water in half. Drank four cups. Starting to feel a little disoriented from lack of sleep. Our other children have noticed I'm a little grumpier than usual.

Day 3—Dazed: No sleep again. Can't make the coffee fast enough. Filled our water softener with coffee grounds instead of salt. Now we have java coming out of every fixture in the house. Beginning to hallucinate from lack of sleep. Had a great conversation with the toaster oven. Seems she has a crush on our George Foreman Grill.

Decided I should get some other chores done since I'm awake—although not coherent. Watered all the plastic plants in the house. Sent our dishes outside and put the cat in the dishwasher. Didn't realize we had a cat.

Day 4—Zombie-like: Annie was up again all night. Called the water softener company to see if they had a unit that makes espresso. Fell asleep for about an hour. Dreamt I was sailing in the new world with Christopher Columbus. Three ships were making the trip: The *Niña*, the *Pinta*, and the *Anna Maria*. The *Anna Maria*'s sails were huge diapers. I was in charge of swabbing the poop deck. Called the water softener company and told them I'd pay for rush delivery. Received a call from our neighbor asking if I had seen his cat.

Day 5—Comatose: No sleep again. Can't stay awake a minute longer. Resorted to putting a fistful of coffee grinds between my cheek and gum. Mmmmmmm. Genuine coffee pleasure without the annoyance of holding a mug. My eyes are as red as radishes, and I haven't shaved since Annie was born. When I answered the doorbell today, the two Girl Scouts selling cookies dropped their wares and ran in terror.

Received a phone call from the president of a major coffee company who said I was chosen as customer of the year and would receive a lifetime supply of coffee. Told him that I had already consumed a lifetime supply of coffee in the past five days.

Took an "Are You Sleep Deprived?" quiz I found in a supermarket tabloid.

1. Do you need an alarm clock in order to wake up at the appropriate time?
   No. To wake up, I'd have to first be asleep.
2. Do you have trouble remembering?
   Yes, especially my name and where I live.
3. Do you often fall asleep while doing other activities?
   ZZZzzzzzzz . . .

Then one night—botta bing, botta boom—Annie slept for eight straight hours. It seemed like a miracle. Our prayers had been answered.

"Botta bing, botta boom" is a term people use when they really mean, "I have no idea what happened, but I suspect a higher power was involved." For example, while the creation of the world took six days to complete, it can be summarized in just fourteen words: In the beginning was God, then—botta bing, botta boom—there was everything else. This is known as the Botta Bing, Botta Boom Theory of Creation—not to be confused with the Big Bang Theory, which was much louder and would have awakened the neighbors if they had already been created.

Some "botta bing, botta boom" moments are more spectacular than others. Being a parent changes your perspective about what constitutes a miracle. Before my wife and I had kids, I rarely thought about miracles. Now that we have three children—Maria (age seven), Paul (age five), and Annie (age two)—I experience miracles all the time, even if they are what some people would consider the minor variety.

If I had to list the top three miracles of all time, they would be the creation of the world, the parting of the Red Sea, and my son's potty training. You might question whether my son's learning to use the john is really in the same category with the creation of the world. I'll admit, I pondered that question for quite a while too. Then I realized the key difference: God didn't have to bribe the world into existing using M&Ms or sit next to Adam for hours reading *The Little Engine That Could* to coax Eve into popping out of Adam's rib.

When our son was two, and my wife and I had cleaned pee off the kitchen floor for the tenth time because he wasn't able to make it to the bathroom, potty training began to appear as miraculous and unlikely as the parting of the Red Sea. And, when the wonderful day arrived and he put on his first pair of "big boy" underwear, we thanked God as if we had just escaped from bondage, which in a sense we had. Our bondage just came in the form of size five Pampers instead of Pharaoh. Potty training may be a minor miracle, but it's still a miracle if you have eyes to see it.

When I was in kindergarten, I prayed for proof that God existed. I wasn't looking for God to reveal himself through the biggest miracle. I was only five, so I was practical. I wanted God to place some graham crackers in a plastic bag in my coat pocket. Every day when I went into the coatroom, I dug my hands down deep into my pockets—but they were always empty. When I graduated to first grade, I gave up asking God for graham crackers because I was convinced he wasn't going to produce.

Thirty-five years passed. Then one day, I put my

hand in my pocket and felt a plastic bag. I pulled it out, and there in the bottom of the bag were three graham crackers. Sure, they belonged to one of my kids, but who's to say God didn't just take the slow fulfillment route—using my daughter as the delivery girl—to grant my kindergarten prayer?

But that wasn't all. As I dug my hand deeper into my coat pocket, I discovered two rubber bands, a dandelion, some pebbles, and a Happy Meal prize. When God answers prayers, he does it in abundance. I showed these treasures to a friend, who showed me the contents of his pocket—two licorice sticks, three pennies, and a feather. I didn't have to ask him what he prayed for in kindergarten.

Minor miracles aren't as glamorous as their larger counterparts, but they have a powerful impact on life. It's no small event when your daughter rides her bike without training wheels for the first time, or your new baby sleeps through the entire night. God uses minor miracles the way we use M&Ms for potty training. He coaxes us along through life with them. Minor miracles are God's way of reading *The Little Engine That Could* to us.

And, now that my eyes have been opened to minor miracles, they arrive on a daily basis.

Epiphany!

VICKI P. GRAHAM

Our son, Nik, his wife, and their brand-new baby girl were spending the weekend at our lake cabin for a much needed rest following the labor and delivery of their first child.

Normally an upbeat, optimistic person, I had for weeks fought off dark thoughts about Nik and his health and safety, partly because he had strayed from his church upbringing, and I felt he was out of his heavenly Father's will. Late at night I would hear horrendous sounds of crashing and the shrill screams of sirens. I knew those were all in my mind and not necessarily premonitions. Nevertheless, I would pray as only a worried mother can, for Nik's well-being, especially considering the imminent arrival of his baby. So I was almost not surprised when the visit every parent dreads arrived at our home.

"Do you have a son named John Nikolas?" asked the policeman who had knocked on our door well after midnight.

"Well, yes, why?" I stammered, rubbing the sleep

from my eyes. My husband stood behind me supporting my shoulders.

The policeman hesitated, then spoke more to my husband than to me.

"We believe your son is the victim in a car wreck, and the only ID we could find was a letter that had the partial address and the name John Nikolas. The car is so destroyed that the state troopers haven't been able to find registration or insurance papers yet."

The officer went on to tell us the car had skidded off the highway near Lake Texoma and had flipped end over end for nearly a hundred yards. Nik had been pulled out of the wreckage and transported by ambulance to the nearest hospital.

Our hearts stopped at his next statement: "We're hoping you can fill in the blanks for us," he said. "An infant seat and a diaper bag were thrown from the car as it rotated, and we're terrified there may have been a baby thrown out.

"But we haven't found a body," he added quickly when he saw our fear. "We're hoping your son was the only one in the car, but we don't know who to contact."

We were frantic because our cabin is very isolated and hard to find. Somebody needed to go there immediately and confirm that the new mother and baby were safe. It was a sixty-mile drive for us, but of course we would start for the hospital right away.

The police officer called the state troopers at the scene and put me on the phone to explain directions to the cabin so a trooper could check since the wreck location was only a few miles away. The officer then offered to escort us to the county line so we could speed to the hospital, and another patrolman would meet us there to lead us the rest of the way. Unfortunately, he didn't know the status of Nik's injuries except that when the medics finally pried him out of the wreckage, he was still alive.

As we hurtled along the highway behind the flashing lights, we prayed fervently, for Nik, and for his wife and baby not to have been passengers. We shouted every Scripture we knew that binds up fear and resists the devil. We praised God for working this horror to the good and that surely He was in control.

We clung to each other and to our faith as we entered the hospital emergency room and heard Nik screaming in pain. His injuries were severe; his left arm and shoulder had been completely pulled away and were hanging, literally, by just his skin. He had multiple head and leg injuries. And he was wild. The doctors explained he was in trauma and not really conscious. They were attempting to stabilize him enough to transport him to a larger hospital that had head and orthopedic specialists waiting Nik's arrival. But they wouldn't promise he would make it.

The good news was, the troopers had located the

cabin and found mother and baby safe. Because the baby was only twelve days old, Nik's wife agreed to stay there with the baby while my husband and I followed the ambulance to the next trauma center. She was a preacher's daughter and promised she would hit her knees and plead for Nik until she got some new word. The cabin had no phone, we were speaking to her on the trooper's cell, so we assured her we would get word to some relatives to come and stay with her.

We didn't think the situation could be worse, but when we careened into the parking lot at the trauma center, the scene was even more gruesome than our experience back at the rural hospital. Lights were flashing, emergency workers seemed to be running everywhere, male nurses struggled to hold Nik down while they moved his gurney to the ER. A team of doctors, already gowned and masked, were waiting by the surgical table. They told us to wait outside.

We were pacing the sidewalk praying fiercely when a doctor came out and got our attention.

"If you believe in prayer, do it mightily, right now." he said. "This is going to be touch and go. And please know," he added kindly, "we're praying for your son too."

It seemed like hours but was only minutes before the same doctor came outside again. "We are treating your son for pain, but we don't dare give him anesthesia till we know the state of his brain. We need you to come in and talk to him or whatever you can do to keep him conscious while we work on him.

Gowned in scrubs, we stood at the head of the surgery table, urged Nik to stay awake, to focus, to not give up. We laid hands on him, we prayed out loud. Occasionally a doctor would mutter, "Amen."

Finally the doctors laid down their instruments and gathered in a corner of the operating room to consult. After much discussion, one came to us and reported the team thought they had Nik stabilized and they would know more in a few hours. Nik would need major surgery on his arm and shoulder but they wanted to put it off until he was stronger and past the crisis. They were moving him to the intensive care unit where he would be watched for twenty-four hours and where we could see him once an hour.

"Thank You, God; thank You, Lord," we said through our tears, "Surely You are working this to Nik's good."

We were relieved even more when our preacher arrived to offer his prayers, and the relatives began to pour in to support us. The next day, Nik's wife was able to visit him and had had enough time to get over her anger at his reckless driving. She was so grateful that he hadn't been killed that she was able to encourage him, and to inform him the baby was thriving.

But it would be two weeks before Nik would get to see his newborn since she wasn't allowed in the hospital.

He went through two extensive surgeries, was encased in a mammoth body cast with his left arm extended at a 90-degree angle from his body, and still suffered extreme pain. And he was acutely depressed from the guilt he suffered over the wreck and the trauma he had caused the family.

Many tears and many days later he was released from the hospital and sent home to recuperate. He was angry, too, at himself and at his dependence on his wife and us to help him get around. He couldn't even dress himself.

Meanwhile, pictures arrived from the state troopers of his demolished car. Looking at the incredibly wrecked pile of metal, Nik experienced an epiphany. He suddenly realized he should have been dead. He realized he needed something; to forgive himself, to seek forgiveness from others, to be shown what to do next. We encouraged him to come with us to church, but he wouldn't hear of it.

A month or so later, my husband and I were at a night church service where we had a guest preacher. He was saying all the things Nik needed to hear. I leaned over to my husband and whispered, "I wish Nik were here. He needs this message of hope."

Just then the preacher stopped his message and walked down to below the podium. His next words made me even sadder that our son wasn't in attendance.

"There is someone here who has lost the use of his

left arm and is in severe depression," he said. "I want you to come down here right now and let me pray for you."

There was a hush as everyone waited to see who would respond. There was a murmur from the crowd as a tall blond rose from the back and limped down the aisle. I turned to see and couldn't believe my eyes. It was Nik! Whatever had moved him, he had talked his wife into driving him to the church meeting. He bravely stood in front of that preacher and received his prayer and blessings. We were all in tears. It was a miracle, not only that he had chosen to come to church, but that the visiting preacher called out the exact description of Nik's injuries and depression.

The cloud was lifted, Nik was a changed young man. But God didn't stop there. Because of his injuries, Nik could no longer do the electronic installations that had been his job since high school. God took care of that. Nik was awarded a full scholarship to university through the state rehabilitation program. Five years later he graduated with full honors with his degree in electrical engineering and a great job awaiting.

Our God is an awesome God!

CHAPTER 5

Finding Hope Through Despair

May the God of hope fill you with all joy and peace as you trust in him, so that you may overflow with hope by the power of the Holy Spirit. (Romans 15:13, NIV)

Hope is the expectation of receiving something good in the future. It's not just a wish or a dream. Instead, it's something you have every reason to believe can happen for you. Sometimes hope comes from unusual sources in our lives, and one of the most unusual places it emanates from is despair. That probably sounds strange, but so often despair leads us to God out of sheer desperation, and God Himself is the divine author and giver of hope. So, no matter what happens in life, hold on to God, and you'll never be without hope.

Peace, Be Still

NIKA MAPLES

Dream: To replace Diane Sawyer on *Prime Time Live.*"

I am smiling beside those words in my high school yearbook. I was absolutely sure where I was going then. After being elected Most Likely to Succeed, I knew that my friends were sure, too.

University journalism courses were a thrill. By my sophomore year in college, I was volunteering at the campus radio station and writing for the school newspaper. I laughed with friends over countless cafeteria dinners when, inevitably, someone would turn on the television set across the room. The evening news turned my head. *That is going to be me,* I thought. *That is going to be me someday.*

Late-breaking news flash.

"Excuse Me," Jehovah said, tapping me on a cold shoulder. "May I have your attention, please?"

I have loved God, worshiped Him, from my first memories of singing "Blue Skies and Rainbows" in vacation Bible school. I have not always, however, actively sought His will in the decisions of my life, whether major or minor. I have not always listened and waited for His voice.

Elijah heard deity in a gentle whisper when he was still enough to listen. *Why couldn't God have spoken up a bit?* I have mused on occasion. Apparently, His servant's stillness was the integral factor in his being heard. Elijah had to be quiet.

"Be still," God said to me. I blustered on in my sophomoric storm.

"Be still."

I was a member of a social club. I waited tables at a local Italian restaurant. I had a small part in an annual variety show. I spent my free time with my boyfriend. I juggled eighteen hours of coursework. There was the radio station. There was the newspaper. There was church. My storm became a category four hurricane, and I could not hear God.

"Peace. Be still," He insisted. "Be still."

And I was.

Six weeks after my twentieth birthday, I suddenly fell to my face on the carpet of my bedroom, unable to move. Lupus, an autoimmune disorder, had caused a massive brain injury, and in the time it takes to turn a radio dial, I became a quadriplegic. Just the week before, I had purchased new running shoes.

In the intensive care unit, I overheard physicians warning of the worst: I may have as few as forty-eight hours left to live. Dear friends and family clung to my quiet hands, caressing limp fingers, and offering disbelieving good-byes. I felt their tears fall on my arms and run down my wrists. Conscious, I would mark the passage of time by the regularity of my heart monitor. I could not speak. I could not open my eyes.

This is suffering, I declared. *This is suffering,* I said to God. I talked to Him and Him alone, day after excruciating day. I continually asked my only Friend, why?

"I consider that [your] present sufferings are not worth comparing with the glory that will be revealed in [you]," he answered (Romans 8:18, NIV).

I had memorized that verse in seventh grade Bible class, not knowing what it meant. What did I understand of glory then? What did I know of suffering? I had tucked the verse away in my heart. God was packing my spiritual suitcase for a journey across the Valley of the Shadow of Death. When those words resurfaced I was quiet and ready to hear His whisper.

"Not worth comparing," He said as He came close.

"Not worth comparing," the words felt like breath on the back of my neck.

"Not worth comparing," I began to say as weeks passed.

My radio frequency finally was tuned in to God, and I listened. Acquaintance with suffering intensified; the characteristics of glory ever deepened in mystery.

Him. Glory is God Himself. Glory revealed in us is

not so much the hope of heaven or miracles wondrously unfurled in our lives, but the majesty of the moment when our suffering quiets us into submission, and we realize that the Creator deigns to live inside the created. We, who are a little hard of hearing, have a front-row seat at the symphony.

My future, my destiny, I have discovered, never was a successful career, but Him. My purpose is God. I live, I am, and yes, I move, for Him.

At one time, every dream I had treasured was irreparably broken. Storm wreckage. But amidst the rain and ruin I was at peace for the first time. In the center, I was still.

A decade now distances me from those early hospital days, and doctors are astonished by my recovery. After months of grueling speech and physical therapy, I eventually regained the ability to speak well and to walk with a prominent limp and a cane. My youthful dreams of delivering the nightly news are all but abandoned. It is a greater honor to deliver the Good News around the world. I have shared the story of God's glory displayed in my life in countries such as Japan, Australia, Germany, Canada, and Thailand. I even taught the children of missionaries in Bangkok for almost a year.

My dearest ministry today is teaching in a public high school. I earned my degree in journalism after all, and I use it to teach English, photojournalism, and creative writing. On the first day of school, I always tell my students about the day I fell to the carpet, so many years ago. Mouths gape, eyes widen, and teenagers sit enrapt; they cannot believe how far I have come. I pray often that my example shines with the likeness of Christ, even though they may not hear the fullness of my testimony in English class.

Mirroring God has become my career plan, my life goal. Sometimes I look into the sweet faces of my students, while reminding them that life can be lost in a moment, and I am overwhelmed with blessing. A God-centered life is the highest call for living, and I would not want to be living anything less.

Running the Race

SUSAN BROOKS

The alarm buzzed like an angry bee in my ear. *Not already,* I thought. But I knew I had to give in. Five A.M.—my new schedule, thanks to my strict training partner for the 2002 Dallas White Rock Marathon. He and I intended to run the marathon in Boston that year, and competing in the Texas race was part of prequalifying. I ran for an hour in the mornings before heading off to my job as a legal secretary. No more stalling. I threw back the covers and reached for my sweats.

I liked setting tough goals for myself. As a runner, I wanted to be the best. As a mom too. I was raising three young girls alone, and I wanted them to be proud of me. I also prayed hard, if not consistently, because I had goals for my spiritual life too. But so far I was having more success in my running life. I hoped God would be patient with me. First things first, and right now I was focused on my girls and the race. There was plenty of time to grow spiritually.

"A quick sprint and some hill work," I said in the mirror, splashing cold water on my face. I'd come back and wake the girls and then take my shower. Now that I was awake, my adrenaline was working. Who cared about breakfast? I looked forward to getting outside. I'd been running since seventh grade and had won some decent medals in college. But I'd never trained so hard before now. My partner's program was relentless, and I was out to prove I was up to the task. "Looking good," he said, pacing me at my side, keeping me going.

Back at home my daughters were up and getting ready for school, and I took a fast shower, thinking about the work on my desk. My schedule was tough there too. I turned off the water and reached for a towel. That's all I remember until I woke up on the bathroom floor.

"Mom!" cried my youngest, Katie, kneeling beside me. "What's wrong?"

Why am I lying here? I wondered. My head throbbed with pain, and I touched my face. My hand came away wet, and when I looked at it, I couldn't believe it. Blood. My nose was bleeding like someone had slugged me.

Later, in the doctor's office, I thought that was exactly what I looked like. I'd hit the counter and had to get several stitches. My head ached like crazy. "I should have had breakfast," I admitted to the doctor, and he agreed. He gave me some pain medicine and I went home.

The next morning I woke up at five, wanting to run. But my head pounded, and I stayed in bed. The next day was the same, and the next. I called my doctor.

"Don't run till the headache goes away," he told me.

I kept taking medicine, but the pain didn't stop. At work, it was hard to concentrate. One morning I put on my running clothes. *Push yourself,* I thought. *The headaches will go away.* But it was no use. Three weeks passed with no relief. I'd missed precious training time. I had to face it. I'd never make the marathon. I told my partner I was quitting.

My headaches persisted. Something wasn't right. Finally I had an MRI. "There's a small tumor on your brain," the doctor said. The headaches finally subsided, but a subsequent CAT scan showed that the tumor had worn a hole in my skull. "You've probably had this tumor all your life," the doctor told me. "Chances are it's benign, but we still have to remove it."

My first thought in any crisis was to call my mother. She had always been strong in the face of every challenge. "This is brain surgery, Mom. What if something goes wrong? What if I don't make it? My girls . . ."

"God's angels are with you, Susan," she said calmly. Mom had always claimed her belief in angels was at the center of her strength. I believed in angels, too, but I didn't have her certainty.

"Pray for me," I said. "I need to be strong—like you."

It was very quiet around the dinner table that night after I announced the news. My daughters glanced nervously at me.

"Will they shave your head?" Jessica asked. She was the oldest. Hair was very important.

"Probably," I said, trying to be light. "It will grow back. Every bad haircut does."

Nobody laughed. *God, don't let the girls be afraid for me. Help me not be afraid for myself.*

But even after a biopsy showed the tumor was benign, I couldn't shake my fear. I'd thought life was like a long-distance race. You kept going till you won. What about all the time I thought I had?

I scheduled my surgery during the two weeks in June when the girls would be visiting their father. The night before the operation, I repeated what my mother had assured me with such certainty: "God's angels are with me. God's angels are with me." I took out pen and paper and wrote a letter to each of my daughters, telling them how much I loved them and believed in them.

"Angels will always be with you," I wrote. By the time I'd written it for the third time, I actually believed it with all my heart. Angels are with us, no matter what happens. I talked to Mom before I went to bed that night. She said she could hear the change in my voice.

I have no memory of the surgery. In two days I was back at home. Mom stayed with me. She made sure I got plenty of rest. When the girls came back from their dad's, it was time for their sleep-away summer camp. In the evenings I drove to the camp to visit them. Their friends knew about my surgery, but all they could talk about were the dark stitches down the left side of my face and my hair. "I guess I look like the bride of Frankenstein," I joked. We laughed together. Technicians had shaved my temple and ten round spots on my head to attach the electrodes. "It's the latest style," I said. "I may keep it." The girls and their friends all giggled.

I surprised myself. This relaxed schedule was a whole new world for me, and I fell into it with ease. A month after the surgery I went back to work. Even then I didn't stress out over the stacks of files on my desk. I didn't think about training. I didn't think about marathons. I didn't think about proving myself. I felt calm inside.

Angels could do that for a person, I guessed. Even me! Eventually I started running again, but I don't have to be the best anymore. I'd just as soon watch the Boston Marathon on television. My daughters are proud of me anyway. Stopping to think about the end of my life has helped me live it more fully. It's not a race but a journey.

A Child-Sized Miracle

JAMI JARNIGAN BEAVERS

My husband, Bryan, was sick Sunday and Monday with the stomach flu that our son Colton had brought home from school the week before. On Tuesday I woke up feeling incredibly nauseous and absolutely terrible. But I had to go to work I knew it was now my turn with this illness that seemed to be sweeping our school system and city. All I really wanted to do was stay in bed and moan.

I told our two small sons how I really needed them to help me that day because their daddy was going out of town for his business and mommy didn't feel well.

When I picked Braxton and Colton up from school that afternoon and we were driving home, five-year-old Braxton asked me how I was feeling. I told him my stomach still hurt and I was still sick.

"Mom," said Braxton, "I'm going to pray for you." He bowed his little head right there in the back seat of the car and just started praying to God to make his mommy feel better and to never let me get sick again. It was the sweetest and most precious little prayer, yet very grown up and confident.

The next morning as we were driving to school, he asked me if I was feeling better. I told him I was, and he got the biggest smile on his face. You could absolutely see the light bulb go on. He was beaming from ear to ear.

"Mom," Braxton shouted, "God answered my prayer!"

How sweet is that? I've never been so excited about being sick in my life. What an awesome lesson for that five-year-old to learn. And my faith is uplifted, too. God really does listen to little children. Thank you, God!

Saved Twice

CARLY BOOHM

"Now remember, you're to stay out of the river," my mom reminded me for the hundredth time as I left that morning.

"Don't worry, Mom," I said before driving off to meet my friends in the church parking lot. My youth leader and several friends from my youth group were heading to the Wenatchee River to take part in a relay race. I wasn't going to be in the race—I'd never even been in a canoe before. My job was to take the canoes and paddles from point to point along the river in the car.

When we arrived at the river, someone suggested we go canoeing. My friends weren't experienced whitewater canoeists, but they had some canoeing experience. Besides, we'd only be floating for about two miles. So I called my mom and asked for permission. After I told her we were going to put the canoes into the water right in front of a park, she reluctantly agreed.

I carefully stepped into the aluminum canoe along with Ruben and Marya—two of my best friends. Excited, we pushed off from shore and began what was supposed to be a short trip. But the rushing water was higher than usual because of heavy rains and melting snow from the surrounding mountains.

We hadn't gone far before the canoe overturned, dumping us into the freezing water. Although the swift current quickly pulled us downriver, we were able to swim to a little sandy island, and Ruben pushed the canoe to shore.

I was shivering and scared and didn't want to get back into the canoe. But we still needed to get back to the other side of the river, where we'd started. And since we'd never be able to swim across the swift waters, the canoe was our only choice.

"Come on, Carly," Ruben insisted.

Reluctantly I climbed back in, and we started down the river. As we approached a bridge, we suddenly turned sideways. Ruben shouted to Marya to paddle harder, but we were sucked toward a pillar of the bridge. We hit it hard, and the canoe capsized, throwing Ruben and Marya into the river.

The force of the water wrapped the overturned canoe around the pillar like tinfoil, and I was pinned about three feet underwater. I couldn't break free or raise my head above the water. My lungs ached for air. I was trapped.

"Please, God, save me."

Ruben and Marya were swept downriver, and as soon as they were able to struggle to shore, they began screaming for help. I managed to lift my hand in a plea for help. Shocked bystanders on the bridge could barely see it above the rushing water. Someone called 911.

It was 2:50 in the afternoon. A frantic race to save my life began.

Meanwhile, Everett Gahringer, a volunteer for the sheriff's department, was running his boat upriver. He saw people on the bridge frantically pointing at me and the submerged canoe.

I was drowning. "Please, God, save me," I prayed. "Don't let me die."

Mr. Gahringer wrapped a rope around the canoe and tugged, hoping to jar me free. But it was useless.

Another sheriff's boat arrived—one with a much more powerful motor. But the river was too strong. Mr. Gahringer went to shore, thinking it was over.

It was now 3:15, and I had been underwater for twenty-five minutes.

Everyone thought it was too late to save me—except for one medic on shore who had been praying. That medic, Shawn Ballard, knew the icy waters would slow my body functions, which would extend my chances of surviving. He knew I might be able to go a little longer without air.

"Let's try again," Mr. Ballard yelled through cupped hands.

Then a fire truck with a winch and cable rolled onto the bridge. Volunteers wrapped the cable around the canoe. Slowly the canoe rose, and my body was freed—only to be swept quickly downriver. Mr. Gahringer revved his motor and raced downstream and was able to pull me into his boat.

It had been forty-five minutes since our canoe had flipped and trapped me underwater. I still wasn't breathing, and my heart had stopped.

Inside the ambulance, Mr. Ballart used shock pads to restart my heart. Several times. It started . . . stopped. Started . . . stopped. "God, please save this girl," he prayed.

My body temperature was 72 degrees when I arrived at the hospital.

My parents drove four hours to the hospital, praying the whole way. When they walked into the intensive care room, I was still unconscious. The doctors told them I probably wouldn't live through the night and if I did, I'd be little more than a vegetable.

But four days later I slowly raised my arm and waved to my mom, who was sitting by my hospital bed.

Whenever people hear my story, they talk about what a miracle it is that I'm alive. The governor of Washington named me the "Miracle of the Season." Larry King interviewed me on his television program, and my story has been on *Dateline NBC,* the *Today* show, and the *It's a Miracle* program.

And it's true: the fact that I am alive is a miracle.

My pre-accident plans to enter the medical field have

not become a career, but I find a lot of gratification volunteering in the pediatric unit of our local hospital. I have gained a deeper compassion for people due to my own struggles in hospitals and back at school. This empathy is not only for people who have been injured, but also for people who become frustrated with studying. I used to think it was easy to get high marks on report cards. Now I realize how much work I have to put into learning new things. Learning new job skills has been very challenging, but giving up is not an option for me.

My day job is taking care of infants at a daycare. They are beautiful reminders of the continuation of life. I may not fulfill my earlier dreams, but I can find joy in what each day brings me and have the hope for a wonderful future of unexpected experiences, close friendships, and God's love and blessings.

I've always shared my faith in Jesus and invited people to come to church with me, but I've had a lot more opportunities to talk to others about Him since the accident. My dad says God spared my life so I can tell others about His love. So I try to do that whenever I can.

When somebody becomes a Christian, people say they got "saved." I like to think God has saved me not just once, but twice.

What Connects Us

JOEL FISHKIN

It was never easy to see my daughter, Samantha, leave for school in the fall. Never easy to have her drive cross-country to Oregon; for her mother, Linda, and me to go another year with our twenty-year-old daughter living three time zones away. And no matter how often Linda and I wrote, called, or thought of her, nothing could replace Sam's free spirit breezing through our days, leaving in her wake a house full of her paintings, her sculptures, and her beautiful music that she composed and played on the piano in our living room.

Sam and a friend backed out of our driveway in Orange, Connecticut, and set out early that August for their senior year at Lewis & Clark College. I stood with Linda in the yard, waving, my wife saying a quiet prayer for their safety.

They'd be going by way of Texas to visit friends and promised to check in with us along the way. We were due a call when Sam's traveling companion reached my wife from outside Fort Worth. The trembling voice on the phone delivered the worst news a parent can ever dread hearing: "There's been a bad accident."

My knees buckled when Linda relayed the call to me at the small manufacturing company I own. I leaned against my desk as my wife told me that Sam had unfastened her seat belt to get a map off the floor when they hit another car full speed. She was hurled through the windshield, landing one hundred feet from the crash. They rushed her by helicopter to the trauma center at Harris Methodist Hospital in Fort Worth.

When Linda phoned the hospital, the chaplain told her, "You should get down here as soon as possible. Your daughter is in a deep coma. They're going to have to operate."

My wife is an emergency-room nurse, so we knew enough about hospital protocol to realize why a chaplain had been chosen to give us that message. I made arrangements at work and drove home immediately while Linda called our son, Chris, at work and arranged our flights.

When we arrived at the hospital in Fort Worth, Sam was in the middle of what would be eleven hours of surgery. A doctor spoke with us in the waiting room. "It was touch and go in the ER," he said, "but she's stabilized enough now to begin surgery."

"What's her condition?" my wife asked. "I'm an RN. You can be open with us."

"Please," I said, "we need to know."

"Samantha," the doctor began slowly, "was barely alive when they got her here. Every bone in her face has been fractured, her right eye may be lost, her palate is split open, and there is a skull fracture that has exposed her brain." He explained that their first priority had been to get air into her lungs.

"I should get back," he told us, standing up to leave. "There are two surgical teams—neurologic and orthopedic—working to put her back together. You can call the scrub nurse for updates."

We appreciated his frankness, but the gravity of Sam's injuries set in and overwhelmed us. It all seemed like some nightmare we were struggling to wake from, our Samantha with severe brain injuries, broken and still unable to breathe for herself. Finally, after six more hours of my pacing and Linda praying, the scrub nurse called to inform us Sam had come out of surgery with a strong heartbeat. "She's still in a deep coma," the nurse told us, "but she's holding her own now."

When we first saw Sam, she lay in intensive care, in a tangle of wires, machines, and intravenous drips. I couldn't believe our daughter was somewhere under all those bandages and tubes, but there sat her small, pale hand atop the covers. I gently reached for it as I tried in vain to hold back my tears.

Linda, with her deep faith, was praying over Samantha.

I had never really prayed before, never done more than keep the major Jewish holidays. Prayer seemed out of place in the matter-of-fact life I led. I just never thought of it as something that could help me. I never felt a need to try speaking to God. Standing in that hospital unit, though, I found myself hoping that my wife had a stronger bond with God than I'd ever managed to forge.

Three days passed with us sleeping in the waiting room, watching over Sam, but still there was no change: heartbeat steady but few other positive signs. We checked into a nearby motel and took shifts at her bedside. We waited and waited for the tiniest flicker of a reaction.

I began talking to Sam. "Everything will be okay," I reassured her. "We're here for you. A lot of people are pulling for you. You should see all the flowers and cards!"

I read to her from her favorite books, played music for her—classic rock from the radio, Paul Simon, Billy Joel, cassettes of her own piano compositions, tapes her friends sent—and I told her how she was in good hands.

The days stretched into a week without any real response; so we found a small apartment in the neighborhood and continued our vigil.

Into the second week, I had to go back home to my business. Our son was able to transfer his job to Texas; so at least Sam had her mom and brother with her. In truth, everyone lent their support—co-workers, friends, schoolmates, family—sending notes, offering prayers, making calls.

I flew back to Fort Worth every weekend. In the meantime, Linda would phone to tell me each day's progress. I hated being away from Sam, especially as she underwent five more operations over the following weeks. Finally, Linda called to say Sam had been moved out of the intensive care unit and into a regular room. She'd been unconscious for almost a month before she showed some minor responses: a slight pressure from her fingers in response to Linda's touch, a small movement when someone came into the room, a fluttery opening of her undamaged eye.

The doctors didn't think Sam was actually seeing anything, but I didn't want to miss any chances. The Friday after Sam was moved into her own room, I flew to Fort Worth and brought her a small chalkboard. I began writing to her—Sam, hello, love—and drew a tic-tac-toe game. She didn't show any reaction.

That Saturday night in our subleased apartment, I returned some calls, one to an old friend in Chicago. He mentioned that his wife had sent Samantha's story to a church prayer network. "This Sunday morning," he said, "a lot of people will be praying for your daughter—thousands, every member of that church, in fact."

"We'll take all the help we can get," I said, asking him to thank his wife for her concern. But as I hung up,

I couldn't help thinking that Linda had been praying since the accident and little had happened. After getting ready for bed, I admitted to Linda that the prospect of a few more prayers tomorrow didn't stir me or fill me with great hope.

"What time are they going to be praying, Joel?" she asked. "I'd like to join them."

The next morning, Linda stayed behind while Chris and I went to see Sam. We both stopped right at the threshold of Sam's hospital room: something about the air of the room was different, the atmosphere changed. Chris and I looked at each other for a second and then edged into the room, going over to Sam. Her eye stayed open and attentive to us standing there.

I grabbed the blackboard and drew a tic-tac-toe grid, placing an O in one box. Chris and I looked expectantly at Samantha. For an instant it seemed all the air had left the room. We both stood absolutely still, silent. Then slowly, but with obvious certainty, Samantha raised her arm to point out where she wanted her X.

I quickly wrote another O and waited as she raised her arm again to her next square. For her final move, Sam took the chalk and drew a rough diagonal through her winning line, my hands trembling as I held the chalkboard.

Chris yelled to the nurses, "She's back!"

I called Linda at the apartment. "Sam's not only back," I said, "she beat me at tic-tac-toe!"

I could hear Linda crying on the other end of the line and, with the room still charged and buzzing with the energy I felt when I entered it, I stammered to her, "Something's happened in this room—I can feel it."

"It's all those prayers," said Linda.

I looked at Samantha with the chalk still clutched in her hand, but I was unable to say anything. Could it really have been all those prayers, those thousands joining together at an exact moment in time for a specific person in need? An incredible sense of wonder and gratitude enveloped me. *Dear God,* I prayed shakily, the words feeling both strange and familiar to me all at once. *Thank you for hearing those prayers! Thank you for our daughter!*

It was the first genuine prayer of my life. I gazed at the board and the thinly chalked diagonal joining Sam's winning Xs, sensing the network of prayer that connected us all.

Several weeks sped by with Sam progressing almost daily. Three months later, we were able to fly her home to Connecticut, and Sam walked off the plane under her own power.

My prayers, which I now say often, have been part of a long and difficult road. Two years have passed since the accident. Sam has very limited vision in her right eye and there are more operations in the offing, yet she continues to amaze her doctors and therapists at the NYU Brain

Injury Day Treatment Program at The Rusk Institute in New York with her progress. And as I write these words, she is sitting downstairs in our living room, playing the piano. The notes fill the house, and I know Linda is there listening to the beautiful music that our daughter is once again composing.

Not a note is played that doesn't evoke my awe at the power of prayer, be it 25,000 strong like that Sunday morning, or just one simple, heartfelt prayer from a father who loves his daughter more than he can say.

Dear God, thank you for Sam.

Internet Angels

SUSAN FARR FAHNCKE

My sister was twenty-eight years old and dying. Diagnosed with an inoperable brain tumor, Angel would be gone by this summer, we were told. It was April, and the weather outside matched this time in her life. Stormy, winter half over, the promise of spring was on the horizon. It was a time of waiting and anguish, a time of learning to live in peace and coming to terms with the end of life as we had known it. Reeling from both physical pain and the pain of her husband simply walking out of her life, my young sister bore loneliness and sorrow of the deepest magnitude. Hard as I tried, I could not erase her sadness. Our days were spent together with me desperately trying to make her smile and forget, if even for a moment, her deep loneliness.

I run a Web site and send out daily inspirational stories. The members of my "online family" are an amazing group of people. Many have suffered through a great deal. Through their letters and stories, I have come to love these people. They have survived cancer, divorce, homelessness, the death of a child, a spouse, a parent, a sibling, disabling accidents, heartache and pain of every other kind. Somehow, life has a way of creating kindness and compassion in the wake of pain.

I found writing about my sister's illness cathartic, and I shared many of our experiences with my daily list. Through my stories, Angel became a part of the lives of these gentle and loving people. Gifts and cards began to arrive for my sister. Relationships with people all over the world developed. As the tumor grew and my sister's ability to communicate, to walk—to live—deteriorated, hundreds of letters and cards, and most of all, prayers, poured forth. And through it all, as her life slowly seeped away, her spirit began to transform. Being loved can create a miracle.

In the beginning of April, I found an incredible site at www.chemoangels.com. I had no idea that clicking on that link would put my sister's heart back on a path of healing, of love. It opened up a world of kindness that became a rainbow during the last weeks of Angel's life. Daily cards, letters, and packages arrived only two days after I signed Angel up for a "Chemo Angel." She had hundreds of angels who reached out with boundless love and compassion. Between the dear friends Angel made from my Web site family and the Chemo Angels, every day of her life brought surprises of love and friendship. My sister's loneliness began to subside and was replaced with the thousands of strangers—angels—who unconditionally loved her and gave her back her smile.

Each day's mail brought stuffed animals, angels of every size, shape, and type. It brought flower seeds, candles, and inspiring cards that strengthened her faith when she needed it most. Unable to walk to the mailbox, she would eagerly wait until I brought the stacks of love hidden in envelopes—all just for her. Her face, swollen and scarred from the chemotherapy and the many falls she had taken, would at last be filled with light and laughter, a gift from heaven wrapped in the love of strangers.

They didn't know it, but each of these dear people created a haven of reprieve from pain for my sister. Her bedroom was filled with their gifts, constant reminders that she was indeed loved, and that God does send angels to do His work. These angels had a very short time to perform a miracle, but they accomplished it with the flurry of angels' wings and the sparkle of heavenly dust. They showered love on my sister with such intensity and such zest that her loneliness evaporated in their warmth.

The week before she died, Angel and I made a pact. In her halting words, she told me if I would be a Chemo Angel, she would be a "Guardian Chemo Angel." I had already applied and was an "angel in waiting." She was delighted, her blue eyes lighting up as our pact was sealed with tears and a sister-hug.

The following Monday, April 30, Angel's spirit left her body. I felt the deepest aching pain I had ever known. The next few weeks were filled with numbness and heartache, but then tiny miracles began to appear in my mailbox every day. Cards with little angels on the return address labels poured, like a cooling summer rain. Day after day brought hundreds of cards, many with angel pins tucked inside, the prayers of countless angels prodding me to look for the rainbow.

Six weeks after Angel's death, I received an e-mail that made my heart skip a beat. It was my first Chemo Angel assignment. A grin slowly spread across my face as tears simultaneously poured down my cheeks. I knew that this patient was going to have two angels, not just one. I wanted to find just the right way to introduce myself and let her know she had an angel in her corner. I finally hit on the perfect thing. It was an e-card with a beautiful, serene angel, wings spread wide. At the bottom, "An angel is watching over you" was written in elegant lettering.

Excited, I looked up at the photo of my sister, taken before she got sick—when her face retained its full beauty and her eyes sparkled with life. I smiled and let the tears flow as I silently told her I was finally keeping our pact. I wrote a brief introductory note and as I clicked "send," I felt the warmth of a hand on my shoulder. I looked behind me. I was alone. I looked up at Angel's photo, and her eyes seemed to twinkle knowingly back at me. The warmth of her hand remained on my shoulder, and I knew that she was with me as we kept our sister pact to care for someone just as she had been cared for. At last, I could begin to repay the gift that was given to Angel during her last weeks on earth. I was grateful to finally be a Chemo Angel, to finally take part in the miracle of giving unconditional love to someone like my sister. At last I was a Chemo Angel, and Angel was a very special guardian angel. "Internet angeling" had come full circle.

The Most Beautiful Word

ANGILEE WALLACE

Please God, let my son live," I pleaded during the hour-long drive to the hospital. All I knew was that Terry and his friend Lowell "Chubs" had been in a terrible car accident early that Saturday morning in July of 1984. My son was just eighteen with a wife and beautiful six-week-old baby girl, Amber.

Since we had no phone at that time, a neighbor had come over to tell me the hospital was trying to contact us. There had been a bad accident. My husband, Jerry, was out on errands with our other two sons, Perry and George, ages seventeen and ten. Terry's place was about a mile away, so I drove over to break the news to his wife, Sandy. Chub's wife was there also. With a car full of various family members, we sped off to the hospital in a panic.

A cloud of fear and disbelief hung over us all. We prayed unceasingly, pleading for the lives of Terry and Chubs. My shock prevented any tears.

I could not believe this was happening to us. We lived a simple but happy life in a modest, two-bedroom house in Marshall, Arkansas. The two youngest boys lived at home while my daughter, Tammy, and Terry both lived close-by with their spouses. At the time, my husband, Jerry, worked as a mechanic. I had been employed at a shift factory for eight years.

When we reached the hospital, we were told the boys had both been taken by helicopter to Springfield Hospital, a trauma center that was three hours away. We got back into the car for the longest drive of our lives.

At the trauma center, we were taken aside so medical personnel could prepare us. Terry had a brain stem injury. This meant paralysis was a possibility. He had been given medication to reduce his brain swelling, but the swelling still continued.

"There will be machines and a lot of tubes," the nurse explained. "Terry has been given medication for pain and is not awake. It is possible he might be able to hear you, so it is very important that you remain calm. We do not want to upset him further in any way."

As I walked into the room and saw all the tubes and machines, my emotions spilled out. I quickly turned around and stepped back out. Shaking, crying, and gasping for air, I tried hard to get myself under control so I could go back in.

Taking deep breaths to calm myself, I walked over to Terry's bedside. Love and fear overwhelmed me as I looked at my son lying unconscious. Yet, seeing him gave me hope. The only physical sign of the accident was a cut over his eye that required three stitches. Terry's arms were twisting back and forth. "Isn't that good?" I asked the nurse when I saw his arms moving. "He can't be paralyzed if his arms are moving."

The nurse explained to me that twitching arms were a reaction to his brain swelling and it was not a good sign. I swallowed hard but could not stop my tears from flowing. I touched his hand and struggled to keep my voice steady. "Terry, hang in there. I love you and I'm going to be here for you," I whispered.

His wife also touched his hand and talked to him reassuringly. I looked at my boy who had always been so healthy and energetic, lying there with tubes going into him. *This can't be*, I thought. But I could not change reality. I could only pray that Terry would recover.

Chubs did not make it. It was still possible that Terry could die also. For several days the doctors tried in vain to stop his brain from swelling. And day after day the only word was: "We don't know what the extent of his injuries will be."

But whatever kind of life Terry would have, as his mother—the one who gave him life—I would be there for him. For weeks I slept on a couch in a waiting room. Jerry came often with the other kids. Together, we kept praying and reassuring Terry to hang in there.

After a few weeks, Sandy and I worked out a routine

where we took turns being with Terry. Although visiting hours were over at 8 p.m., the nurses let us stay much later. After a couple months, they also let us sleep in the nurses' dorm next to the hospital.

Toward the end of October, the doctor told us that there was no longer any reason to keep Terry in the hospital. He was still in a coma, so he needed to be moved to a nursing home. I had not given up hope, but the doctors could do no more for him.

Terry was placed in a nursing home two hours away from our house. At this point, people started losing hope. Some questioned if perhaps it would have been better for Terry to have died in the accident. If he never came out of the coma, was my desire to keep him alive selfish? I did not want to let him go, and yet, what did Terry want?

I began asking God what He wanted. "Lord, I love Terry and I want You to heal him, but Your will be done," I started praying. "I trust in You, God." In the midst of my pain, I began to feel some peace. If Terry continued to live, it would be because God wanted Him to.

I returned to work, where I had been given a leave of absence, but I spent every other weekend at the nursing home. My mother and sister lived nearby, so I often stayed with them or simply slept in a recliner in Terry's room.

As Christmas neared that first year after the accident,

I could not imagine a family celebration without Terry. I wanted him home. Since he was still in a coma, there was great concern that this would be too difficult. I was scared but I was also determined; Terry needed to be home during Christmas.

Terry's feeding tube was removed shortly after Thanksgiving. I had watched the nurses feed him with a syringe and decided I could manage. Staff from the nursing home helped us carry Terry into the car. Family and friends helped us carry him into the house once we got him home.

In the familiar setting of home and surrounded by family and friends, loved ones came by to wish Terry a merry Christmas. Everyone talked to him as if he were the old Terry. He was still in a coma, but I believe he had to know the difference between being in the nursing home and being at home. I could not prove it, but I felt it with my whole heart.

From that time on, we started bringing Terry home every other weekend. By the end of the next year, Terry was moved into a nursing home in Mountain View, which is the town where I work. I frequently stopped by to see him after work and we brought him home every weekend.

The months turned into years—five, ten, fifteen—and people saw no improvement. Terry's young wife had gotten on with her life. His daughter, Amber, only occasionally saw her father as she grew up. A few people questioned the wisdom of bringing him home every weekend, but most of our family and friends supported us. It was a strain, but Jerry and I were united in our unwavering love for Terry.

Like a bud that blooms so slowly that its movement is imperceptible, Jerry and I felt that our son *was* opening up. It was so gradual, it escaped others. There were little things like a blink or a wink. One day, Terry laughed. And once Terry did something, he could continue to do it.

Driving with Terry in the car one morning, his head bobbed up and down after I asked him a question. I paid no attention, thinking it was the bouncing of the car that caused it. But Jerry cried out: "Look, he's answering you. He's shaking his head yes!" From that moment on, Terry was able to shake his head when asked a question. Later on, he started making the sound: "uh-huh."

Nineteen years after the accident, on Wednesday, June 11, 2003, I walked into Terry's room and said "Hi, Terry," as I always did. One of the nursing home aides asked him, "Who is that, Terry?"

"Mom," he answered clearly. I almost fell over, I was so shocked. The aide and I looked at each other with the same astonished expressions on our faces. Tears of joy rolled down our laughing cheeks as we ran over and hugged Terry.

"Did you hear that?" I cried. "He said 'Mom!' Terry say that again!"

Terry laughed and again said the most beautiful word I had ever heard: "Mom."

Terry did not say another word that day, but after nineteen years, he had spoken! His one word was music to my ears, more incredible than his first "mamma" so many years before. We brought him home for a weekend visit that Friday. I kept asking him questions that he could answer with "Mom." Later that day, I got him to say "Pepsi."

On Saturday morning, I awoke to turn him over at 4 A.M., which was a necessary task. This was always a time when I would talk with him. Terry was mumbling.

"I know you are trying to tell me something," I said. "Just keep trying and I'll catch it," I told him. He kept struggling until "Mom and Dad" tumbled out.

"Say it again," I pleaded excitedly through my tears.

Terry responded: "Mom and Dad."

"Terry, tomorrow is Father's Day," I cried. "When Dad gets up, we'll tell him what you can say. It will be his Father's Day present from you."

When Jerry got up, I could not contain my excitement. "Jerry, Terry has a Father's Day present for you," I said, escorting him to Terry's bedside. Then, very clearly, Terry spoke: "Mom and Dad."

Jerry is not one given to emotions, but tears glistened in his eyes. "That's the best Father's Day present I could have," he said.

For breakfast, I expected Terry to ask for Pepsi—his new word—when I asked him what he wanted to drink. Instead, he said: "Milk."

When a nurse at the nursing home learned of all Terry's words, she arranged for a speech therapist to visit Terry. "Angilee, I believe he will be speaking in full sentences within a week," she announced.

The next week, when I walked into his room, he was telling the people around him that his birthday was April 7, 1964. I laughed and hugged him then asked: "Terry, what else can you say?"

"Anything I want," he answered, laughing.

By the end of August we brought Terry home to stay. I quit my job to care for him full-time. His daughter, Amber, is nineteen now. She comes every day to spend time with her dad. She loves Terry just because he is her dad.

Terry is a quadriplegic as a result of the accident. Yet, many times he has told me, "I'm so happy." God wanted Terry to live and now I know Terry also wanted to survive. My family is still the center of my life, but God is also there with us.

My son's life is a miracle. I keep praying and trusting that God will continue to see us all through.

A NOTE FROM THE EDITORS

This original book was created by the Books and Inspirational Media Division of Guideposts, the world's leading inspirational publisher. Founded in 1945 by Dr. Norman Vincent Peale and his wife, Ruth Stafford Peale, Guideposts helps people from all walks of life achieve their maximum personal and spiritual potential. Guideposts is committed to communicating positive, faith-filled principles for people everywhere to use in successful daily living.

Our publications include award-winning magazines like *Guideposts*, *Angels on Earth*, *Sweet 16*, and *Positive Thinking*, best-selling books, and outreach services that demontrate what can happen when faith and positive thinking are applied to day-to-day life.

For more information, visit us online at www.guideposts.org, call (800) 431-2344, or write Guideposts, 39 Seminary Hill Road, Carmel, New York 10512.